Angry People

Other titles by Warren W. Wiersbe

Living Lessons
FROM GOD'S WORD

Angry People

... and what we can learn from them

Warren W. Wiersbe

Baker Books

A Division of Baker Book House Co
Grand Rapids, Michigan 49516

Published by Baker Books
a division of Baker Book House Company
P.O. Box 6287, Grand Rapids, MI 49516-6287

Previously published in 1987 by the Good News Broadcasting Association, Inc.

Printed in the United States of America

Library of Congress Cataloging-in-Publication Data

Wiersbe, Warren W.
    Angry people : and what we can learn from them / Warren W. Wiersbe.
        p.   cm. — (Living lessons from God's word)
        ISBN 0-8010-6380-9
        1. Anger—Religious aspects—Christianity. 2. Christian life—Biblical teaching. I. Title. II. Series.
    BV4627.A5 W54 2001
    248.4—dc21   2001035943

For current information about all releases from Baker Book House, visit our web site:
                http://www.bakerbooks.com

Contents

Foreword

This book contains ten edited and expanded transcriptions of radio messages I delivered over the Back to the Bible international network.

These messages were first spoken to a listening audience made up of a variety of people in many nations and at many stages of spiritual growth. This explains the brevity, simplicity and directness of the material. Were I writing a commentary or presenting a longer pulpit message, the approach would be vastly different.

In sending out these messages, my prayer is that they will encourage and build up God's people and help them in their own ministries.

Warren W. Wiersbe

1

The Rage within Us

What do Moses, King David, the prophet Jonah, and Jesus Christ all have in common? According to the Scriptures, they all experienced anger. With some, it was righteous anger; with others, their anger was sinful. In anger, Moses broke the two tablets of the Law when he came down from the mountain. David became angry and passed judgment on an unknown criminal, only to discover that *he* was the man. In so doing, he brought heartache upon himself and his family for years to come.

Anger is a fact of life. Everyone experiences this emotion from time to time. Many righteous people in the Bible became angry, including our Lord Himself. For this reason, God's Word has much to say about the subject of anger— what it is and what it can do. When anger is controlled and is displayed according to biblical principles, it can be a positive force that will bring glory to God. When anger is selfish, it can destroy a great deal of what is good. Therefore, it's important that we understand this force and learn to use it in the way God intended.

In this study, we will be examining anger from a biblical perspective, seeking to discover when anger is acceptable to God and what the principles are for controlling it. In studying the many forms of anger, we will be looking at key people in the Scriptures who became angry. As we see how these people handled their anger, we in turn will learn the right and wrong ways for dealing with the rage within us.

Defining Anger

The dictionary tells us that anger is a strong feeling of displeasure aroused by a real or a supposed wrong. This is an apt definition. We have all experienced this strong feeling of displeasure on many occasions. Perhaps someone has almost sideswiped your car on the highway, forcing you off the road. You are furious with the other driver. Why? Because he had no right to drive that way. Or you turn on the news and hear about someone who has been abused by another person. You become indignant because something is not being done about this problem. Our anger can be aroused in an instant by any real or imagined wrong committed against ourselves or others.

Anger is a very strong emotion. When allowed to continue unchecked, anger can destroy the enraged person and others. However, people who deny that they are angry can also be severely hurt. Studies have shown that anger has definite effects on the body. Doctors and counselors are now telling us that suppressed anger can contribute to a number of physical problems and illnesses.

10

Anger itself is not something evil. God has instilled in us certain emotions, including anger. When these emotions are working together properly, they serve to protect us and build us up. Anger is something like fire. When used correctly, fire warms us and helps us cook meals and drive machinery. However, if left to itself, a small fire will soon become a raging inferno, destroying everything in its path. Anger can fuel our emotional defense system when it is used as God has directed, or it can cause a great deal of damage if it's left uncontrolled.

We are created in the image of God—a God who becomes angry at times. However, the anger displayed by our Lord is always righteous anger. This, then, is the key to using and controlling anger. The philosopher Aristotle wrote: "Anybody can become angry. That is easy. But to be angry with the right person and to the right degree and at the right time and for the right purpose and in the right way—that is not within everybody's power and is not easy."

Unfortunately, Aristotle was right. Few people have learned how to express this God-given emotion in the way that He intended. Too often we allow our anger to lead into temptation and sin. When we mix anger with pride, pettiness, envy, or greed, we create serious problems for ourselves and for others. In the lives of David, Jonah, and many others in the Bible, you find many vivid illustrations of the destructive power of sinful anger. However, it's possible to be angry and yet not sin. In Ephesians 4:26 the apostle Paul said, "In your anger do not sin" (see also Ps. 4:4). The Lord Jesus Christ and Moses both became angry without sinning. When we follow their example in using anger properly and righteously, then anger will become a constructive, rather than destructive, force in our lives.

11

Different Kinds of Anger

Is there more than one kind of anger? Yes, and we must learn to identify them. The Bible makes a number of distinctions between types of anger. For instance, in Colossians 3, Paul reminded the believers that they had been raised with the Lord Jesus Christ and therefore should live by heavenly standards. They must abandon certain worldly lifestyles and practices: "But now you must rid yourselves of all such things as these: anger, rage, malice, slander, and filthy language from your lips" (v. 8).

Notice that *anger* is distinguished from *wrath* in this passage because these two aren't identical. In the Greek text, the words translated *anger* and *wrath* are different. The Greek word for *anger (orge)* describes a more settled and lasting inward feeling of anger. It is the type of anger that grows slowly and often leads to revenge. On the other hand, the Greek word translated *wrath (thumos)* indicates a sudden and agitated outburst of anger. Sometimes wrath reflects the ongoing anger that has been smoldering in the heart. Wrath usually flares up suddenly and then quickly subsides. The Bible has much to say about both kinds of anger.

In addition, the Scriptures make a distinction between holy and unholy anger. Many Christians would have a hard time believing that any kind of anger could be holy because they mistakenly consider all anger to be evil. However, keep in mind that God Himself shows anger and that the Bible is filled with references to the wrath of God. Since the Lord is holy, just, and good, He could only express a holy and just anger. Therefore, feeling the emotion of anger is not wrong. Anger can be good and holy when expressed in the same way that the Lord reveals His anger.

Righteous Anger

What constitutes holy anger? First, it is anger toward sin, because God hates sin. If you read the passages that refer to the wrath of God, you will discover that, in each case, God was displaying anger toward sin. When Jesus lashed out against the money changers in the temple, He did so because they were cheating the people and using God's house for personal gain (see Matt. 21:12–13). God wants us to hate sin and to be angry at injustice in our world. Psalm 97:10 tells us, "Let those who love the LORD hate evil. . . ." If we truly love the Lord, we will become angry whenever we see people sinning against Him or against His children.

Second, holy anger is anger that is controlled by God. This kind of anger shows inner strength and self-restraint. Thomas Fuller, a famous Puritan preacher, once described anger as one of the sinews of the soul. Anger that is controlled by God and directed toward His cause will make you a stronger person and give you the courage to do what is right.

Third, holy anger is concerned with defending and building up others rather than protecting our self-esteem. Righteous anger is anger *for* people and not *against* people. It is used as a tool for construction rather than a weapon for destruction. Holy anger is always mixed with a loving concern for people, including people who have hurt us or others.

Finally, holy anger produces righteousness and not unrighteousness. It builds up our Christian life and the work of God. When we harbor unholy anger, it begins to affect every area of our lives. We find it hard to pray; and when we do pray, we're unable to pray with the right motive and for the right things. That's why 1 Timothy 2:8 instructs us to "lift up holy hands in prayer, without anger or disputing."

Holy anger motivates us to share problems and burdens with the Lord because we want His name glorified.

Another area of life that suffers when we feel unholy anger is our Christian service. This is why James 1:19–20 warns us, "Everyone should be quick to listen, slow to speak and slow to become angry, for man's anger does not bring about the righteous life that God desires." When we nurse grudges and feed our selfish anger, we will not be useful to God in accomplishing His will. However, holy anger fans the flames within us and spurs us into action in defending the things of God.

Directions for Controlling Anger

The ability to feel anger is a gift from God. The Lord built anger into our emotional system for our benefit. But, as we have seen, not all anger is good. It depends on how we use it. Anger is extremely powerful; unless it's kept under control, it can be destructive. When anger is allowed to go anywhere it wants to go, it becomes like a river that has overflowed its banks. The normally quiet and peaceful river becomes a raging flood that destroys everything in its path. Thus, learning to control our anger is vital if we are to use it for God's glory and our good. God's Word gives us some specific directions to help us.

First, we must yield to the Holy Spirit. When we do, He will guide us and produce His fruit in our lives: "But the fruit of the Spirit is love, joy, peace, patience, kindness, goodness, faithfulness, gentleness and self-control" (Gal. 5:22–23). The Holy Spirit will not only give us the kind of character that wards off anger, but He will also teach us self-control so that we can keep our anger in check when it arises.

Some people have the mistaken idea that when the Holy Spirit takes control of your life, you have no responsibility for self-control. I have participated in Bible conferences with preachers who did not know how to watch the clock. Consequently, when it was my turn to preach, they had used up fifteen or twenty minutes of my preaching time. What was their excuse? "Well, Brother Wiersbe," they would say, "you know that when the Spirit takes over, you've just got to keep going." However, the Bible teaches me that when the Spirit of God takes over, we gain more self-control, not less. I've noticed in my own life that when the Holy Spirit is in control, I am able to control my words and my time better, completing tasks when they need to be done. In instructing the Corinthian saints regarding the proper use of spiritual gifts, Paul wrote: "The spirits of prophets are subject to the control of prophets. For God is not a God of disorder but of peace" (1 Cor. 14:32–33). If anger is out of control in our lives, then God is not the source of our strength.

The Holy Spirit can fill us with the love, joy, peace, patience, and self-control we need to keep our anger in check and directed toward useful ends. Anger, wrath, envy, and strife are all works of the flesh (see Gal. 5:19–21). But when our anger is under the Spirit's control, then we are able to use it as a tool for building up rather than as a weapon for tearing down.

Second, we not only need the fullness of the Holy Spirit but also humility and honesty. In the Sermon on the Mount, Jesus warned about the dangerous consequences of anger: "You have heard that it was said to the people long ago, 'Do not murder, and anyone who murders will be subject to judgment.' But I tell you that anyone who is angry with his brother will be subject to judgment" (Matt. 5:21–22). The Lord added a special warning: "Therefore, if you are offer-

15

ing your gift at the altar and there remember that your brother has something against you, leave your gift there in front of the altar. First go and be reconciled to your brother; then come and offer your gift" (vv. 23–24). Before we worship God, we must be right with our brother.

So often our anger is unwarranted. We become enraged over some imagined wrong. Christ's words speak to us of the importance of evaluating our angry feelings to see if they are really justified. We need to pray, asking the Lord if we said or did something that offended our brother, and if we are at fault, we must take steps to rectify the problem. We must honestly and humbly go to the person with whom we are angry and seek his or her forgiveness. This isn't easy to do. It's even more difficult to go to someone who has genuinely wronged us and take the first steps toward reconciliation. Our pride tells us, "I'm not going to apologize to him. It was his fault, and he should apologize to me!" However, if we truly want to gain control over our anger, we must develop the kind of humility and honesty that not only admits when we are wrong but also wants to seek peace. Without the right attitude in our hearts, our relationship with the Lord will suffer.

Third, in order to control our anger, we need to be careful how we speak. In Proverbs 15:1 we are told, "A gentle answer turns away wrath, but a harsh word stirs up anger." Conversations are like small fires: The more fuel you add to them, the more they blaze. Nothing cools a person's temper faster than a calm, quiet response. We need to remember that it takes two people to have an argument. Many angry arguments and hurt feelings could be avoided if people would learn to control their tongues. If we are allowing the Holy Spirit to control us, He will give us the ability to speak the truth in love (see Eph. 4:15).

16

Fourth, we need to remember the consequences of anger. One of the best deterrents to uncontrolled anger is simply looking ahead and realizing what will happen if we lose our temper. Proverbs 19:19 states, "A hot-tempered man must pay the penalty; if you rescue him, you will have to do it again." In other words, the person who has an uncontrolled temper, who flares up at the slightest provocation, will constantly create trouble for himself and for others. Angry people say and do things they later regret. However, even though they repent and are truly sorry for the trouble they have caused, they can never undo the damage. The physical and emotional scars they have inflicted will always remain.

We all need a proper perspective with regard to anger, and that perspective is described in Proverbs 19:11: "A man's wisdom gives him patience; it is to his glory to overlook an offense." We need to use discretion and prudence in determining when to become angry and overlook whatever can be safely overlooked. Anger can drain us physically, mentally, and emotionally, and many things people say and do are so trivial that they simply don't deserve the investment of time and energy that anger demands. Proverbs 14:29 tells us, "He who is slow to wrath has great understanding, but he who is impulsive exalts folly" (NKJV).

Uncontrolled anger can damage us even more than it damages other people. That's why it is so important to have a proper perspective toward the things that happen to us. One of the best weapons for controlling anger is a sense of humor. We need to learn to laugh off people's unintentional, rude actions and thoughtless words. Rather than harboring anger and resentment, we need to tell ourselves, "Oh, he didn't mean that" or "Well, she probably didn't realize she was upsetting me." When we see these hurts in the

17

proper light, we won't waste our precious energy nursing needless grudges.

In order to have a proper perspective toward anger, we must develop mature Christian character. The more we become like Christ, the stronger we will be. As Proverbs 16:32 tells us, it takes more strength to subdue our anger than to defeat an entire army: "He who is slow to anger is better than the mighty, and he who rules his spirit, than he who captures a city" (NASB). We have an army that is waging war within us. If we allow the army to revolt, our anger will take over and we will do things we shouldn't do. When we cultivate Christian character, we will learn to forgive as Christ forgives. We will leave our sinful anger at the cross. In Ephesians 4:32, Paul wrote: "Be kind and compassionate to one another, forgiving each other, just as in Christ God forgave you." If someone does something that hurts you and you want to respond in anger, just go to the cross and remember how much God has forgiven you.

Finally, we need to remember that God is the final judge. Romans 12:19 tells us, "Do not take revenge, my friends, but leave room for God's wrath, for it is written: 'It is mine to avenge; I will repay,' says the Lord." Only God has the ability always to judge fairly and act justly. Not only is He aware of our actions, but He also knows the thoughts and motives behind them. A person's appearance and actions can easily deceive us, but not God. Someone who may appear to be our friend could really be our enemy and vice versa. Therefore, we need to leave all judgment to the Lord. Our job is to love those who hurt us: "If your enemy is hungry, feed him; if he is thirsty, give him something to drink. . . . Do not be overcome by evil, but overcome evil with good" (vv. 20–21). This is where faith enters in. When people cause us to be angry and hurt, we must be willing to give the problem to God and trust Him to take care of it.

Anger is a useful gift from God. When this emotion is displayed according to God's directives, it can be a positive force in our lives. However, anger can also be terribly destructive if it is not controlled. May God give us the grace to control the rage within us and to use it for His glory.

2

Moses
ANGER CAN GIVE YOU COURAGE

If you want to get some insight into the character of people, find out what makes them laugh, what makes them weep, and what makes them angry. Not all anger is sinful. When it's displayed for the right reasons and in the right manner, anger can reveal a holy and righteous character.

One of the best examples of righteous anger is found in the life of Moses. Following Israel's miraculous deliverance from Egypt, Moses led the people to the foot of Mount Sinai where God would give them His Law. Moses journeyed up the mountain to receive that Law and to get his instructions from the Lord. As Moses tarried on Mount Sinai for many days, the people became restless and wondered if he would ever return.

They came to Aaron and said, "Come, make us gods who will go before us. As for this fellow Moses who brought us up out of Egypt, we don't know what has happened to him" (Exod. 32:1). Aaron agreed to their foolish request, something he shouldn't have done. He instructed them to bring their gold jewelry and he fashioned all of it into the shape of a calf. He then declared a day of feasting, and the people sacrificed to their golden idol. But the people had forgotten that it was the Lord Jehovah who had brought them out of Egypt, and now they were rejecting Him!

Their sin did not go unnoticed. On the mountain, the Lord told Moses, "Now leave me alone so that my anger may burn against them and that I may destroy them" (v. 10). God even offered to make a new nation with Moses as the founder, but Moses pleaded with the Lord to spare the people. God honored his fervent prayer and forgave the Israelites, but He judged those who rebelled against His Law.

When Moses had finished praying and communing with the Lord, he came down from the mountain. "When Moses approached the camp and saw the calf and the dancing, his anger burned and he threw the tablets out of his hands, breaking them to pieces at the foot of the mountain. And he took the calf they had made and burned it in the fire; then he ground it to powder, scattered it on the water and made the Israelites drink it" (vv. 19–20).

Was Moses justified in his anger? Yes, he was, because he was displaying a righteous anger against sin. When he broke the tablets of the Law, ground the idol to powder, threw the powder into the water, and made the people drink the water, Moses wasn't having a temper tantrum, nor was he merely punishing the people. In these actions, he gave the nation an object lesson to bring the people back to God. He broke the tablets of the Law to show the people how they had broken God's Law and were not worthy to belong to God. He burned the calf and made the people drink it to show them the futility of their idol worship. They had been serving a god who was even weaker than they were, a god whose substance they could drink!

When Moses finished rebuking the people, he called for a new commitment to God, saying, "Whoever is for the LORD, come to me" (v. 26). He then instructed those who had come to mete out the Lord's punishment on those who had not repented, and three thousand people were slain because of their sin.

There are a number of reasons why Moses was justified in his anger. First, he had the right motivation: He was displaying a holy anger against sin. Second, he had a right relationship with God and had prepared himself for the encounter through prayer and worship. Third, he displayed his anger in the right manner so that it was constructive rather than destructive. And fourth, he had the right attitude in his anger. His anger was motivated not out of hatred for people but rather out of love for God and for his nation.

"Indignation grips me because of the wicked, who have forsaken your law" (Ps. 119:53). When Moses saw the people sinning so grievously, he experienced a heartfelt horror and fear for them. Moses' anger wasn't just the deep resentment of a godly leader, but it was indignation that Israel had deliberately broken God's Law. Moses was brokenhearted and filled with anguish. He grieved for the people, just as the psalmist did: "Streams of tears flow from my eyes, for your law is not obeyed" (v. 136). "I look on the faithless with loathing, for they do not obey your word" (v. 158). When our anger is motivated out of loving concern for the sinner and holy respect for the authority of God's Word, God can use it to honor His name. Anger plus love produces anguish, a heart broken because of concern for the people of God and the glory of God.

A closer examination of this incident reveals several considerations that show why Moses was justified in his anger.

23

Who Sinned

If it had been the Canaanites who had made and worshiped a golden calf, we could understand why they did it, because they were idolaters. But the people dancing about the calf and sinning were the children of Israel—God's chosen people!

A pastor was preaching a series of messages on "the sins of the saints." One of the church members approached him and said, "I don't like it when you preach about sin in the lives of believers. After all, sin in the life of a Christian is different from sin in the life of an unsaved person." And wisely the pastor responded, "Yes, it's worse."

When we consider everything the Israelites had received from God, it's hard to understand how they could rebel against Him as they did. They had been chosen by God's grace. God made a covenant with Abraham and promised to make him into a great nation, as numberless as the sands of the sea and the stars of the heavens (see Gen. 12:1–3, 22:17). During years of famine and plenty, bondage and freedom, God's special blessing of provision and protection had been on His chosen people. Even as they sinned against God, they were on their way to the land of abundance that God had promised them. What ingratitude!

Not only did the Israelites have an honored place as God's chosen people, but they had just recently been delivered from the land of Egypt by God's power (see Exodus 12–14). During the years the nation of Israel had lived in Egypt, they were surrounded by idolatry and superstition, and some of that idolatry had remained in their hearts when they left the land. God miraculously delivered them from bondage and they saw the power of God bring Egypt to its knees. God opened the Red Sea to allow Israel to escape on dry ground, and God defeated the enemy army that came to attack them. What more could the Lord have done to prove His power and His love? Yet, in spite of this demonstration of divine power, the Israelites bowed down before an idol that they themselves had made. No wonder Moses was angry!

The children of Israel were also a people whom God was feeding each morning by sending them manna. Whatever supplies the vast multitude of Jews had taken with them from Egypt had long been depleted, but once again God lovingly cared for His children. Each morning they found the ground covered with manna (see Exod. 16). When they were thirsty, He brought water from a rock to meet their needs (see Exod. 17:1–7). The Lord was leading them and feeding them, and what were they doing? Turning against Him!

If all this wasn't enough to warrant their devotion, the Israelites had been included in God's covenant. "Now if you obey me fully and keep my covenant, then out of all nations you will be my treasured possession. Although the whole earth is mine, you will be for me a kingdom of priests and a holy nation" (Exod. 19:5–6). The people had responded piously, "We will do everything the LORD has said" (v. 8), and yet these were the same people who bowed before a golden calf!

The children of Israel had been chosen by God's grace, delivered by God's power, fed by God's goodness, and graciously included in God's covenant. They had promised to obey Him. They were on their way to God's inheritance. Yet they were practicing idolatry and immorality, corrupting themselves and turning away from the Lord, the source of all their blessings. When we consider who had sinned, we can see why Moses' anger was justified.

25

Where They Sinned

If the children of Israel had only stopped to remember who they were and Whose they were, they would never have made such a foolish request of Aaron. But their sin becomes even more grievous when you consider where they were when they sinned. They were at Mount Sinai, where they had received the Law! This included the law forbidding them to make and worship idols (see Exod. 20:4–5). They were an unholy people at a holy mount!

Not only were they at Mount Sinai, but they were in the presence of God. The Lord had appeared on the mountain as a fire and had spoken to the people and given them His Law (see Exod. 19:18–20:21). The fire and thunder and lightning had frightened the Jews and they cried out to Moses for help, but now all of that was forgotten. Later, Moses returned to meet the Lord on the mountain to receive further instructions, and he stayed forty days and nights. While Moses was on the mountain, the glory of the Lord was visible to the children of Israel (see Exod. 24:13–18). Deuteronomy 9:15 informs us that Moses had to go through smoke and fire on his way down to the camp. The children of Israel were in the very presence of God, yet even as they watched the display of His glory on the mountain, they made an idol and bowed down before it. They were at Mount Sinai to receive God's Law, and yet they disobeyed that Law after promising to keep it.

It seems unbelievable that these people could reject God and His Law only days after they had seen His glory and heard His voice. Yet it shows us vividly how weak man really is and how impossible it is for the Law to save us. Romans 8:3 tells us, "For what the law was powerless to do in that it was weakened by the sinful nature, God did by sending his own Son in the likeness of sinful man to be a sin offering. And so he condemned sin in sinful man. . . ." Notice that the Law was not weak; it was sinful human nature that was weak and couldn't obey the Law of God. The children of Israel affirmed their promise to obey God's Law, not realizing that it's impossible for man to obey the Law of God by relying on human strength.

Those who think they can reach heaven by keeping the Ten Commandments or doing good works need to read this account again. Throughout the Old Testament, we find the children of Israel sinning repeatedly, frequently bowing down to idols and committing immorality in the name of pagan religion. The law could not change them or control them; it could only condemn them.

Some people feel that Moses' actions were too harsh, especially since he broke both tablets of the Law when the people had only broken one law. But the writer James clearly tells us, "For whoever keeps the whole law and yet stumbles at just one point is guilty of breaking all of it" (James 2:10). The law can be compared to a chain of ten links. Imagine that you are hanging over a chasm, holding on to this chain. How many links have to break before you will fall? Only one! When the children of Israel broke the one law against idolatry, they were guilty of breaking the whole law. And when we consider that the people of God had just received this law from the Lord Himself, it makes Moses' anger all the more reasonable.

The holy law of God isn't something to trifle with. It can't make us righteous, but it does reveal the righteousness of God.

How They Sinned

In understanding the reasons for Moses' anger and the biblical precedent he set in expressing it, we need to consider not only who was involved and where they were at the time, but also how they sinned. God hates all sin, but probably no sin is more hateful to Him than idolatry. In worshiping the golden calf, the Israelites were not only rejecting God's Law but were rejecting the Lord Himself.

The severity of their sin becomes even more apparent as we consider the object of their worship—a golden calf. We don't know exactly what it looked like, but we do know that it was a molten image made out of gold. I also get the impression that it was engraved. It may not have been a huge image, but it was big enough for the people to see and give homage to. They even put an altar before it and offered sacrifices to it.

Why did the Israelites make their idol in the image of a calf? Probably because the people in Egypt worshiped the calf and so did Israel's neighbors in Canaan. I can imagine the heathen people watching the Israelites and saying, "Those Jews are just like us. They're worshiping a golden calf just as we do. Why, these are our people!" Not only did the children of Israel reject their living Lord, but they lost their testimony. Psalm 106:19–22 tells us how terrible this sin really was: "At Horeb they made a calf and worshiped an idol cast from metal. They exchanged their Glory for an image of a bull, which eats grass. They forgot the God who saved them, who had done great things in Egypt, miracles in the land of Ham and awesome deeds by the Red Sea." The children of Israel turned away from the glory of God they had seen on Mount Sinai, exchanging it for an image of one of His creatures; and men and women have been doing this ever since (see Rom. 1:21–23).

When Moses saw this great sin, he became intensely angry. In his response, we can see the motivation behind his anger: Moses was concerned about the glory of God. He could not bear to see God's glory corrupted and His name scorned. Even in begging God to spare the people, Moses' great concern was the glory of God (see Exod. 32:11–14). He asked the Lord to forgive Israel for the sake of His own glory and His testimony before the heathen nations. Do we have this kind of concern for God's glory today? Do we seek to exalt and defend His great name?

Why They Sinned

Considering the Israelites' favored position with God and everything they had seen Him do in recent months, it is especially hard to understand why they sinned. But Exodus 32:1 gives us the answer: It was their unbelief and impatience. The people didn't trust the Lord implicitly. At the first sign of trouble, their faith wavered. They were unwilling to wait for His will to be revealed. They frequently ran ahead of God and did things their own way.

Their unbelief and impatience were apparent long before they made the golden calf. The Lord originally intended to give the Law to the people directly, but when His voice thundered from the mountain, the people became frightened and told Moses, "We don't want to hear God's voice; we can't stand it. You go speak with the LORD and then come back and tell us what He said" (see Exod. 20:19). So Moses met the Lord on the mountain and the Lord gave him the Ten Commandments and "The Book of the Covenant" which he delivered to the people (Exod. 19:20–23:33). Then Moses returned and God gave him detailed instructions for the construction of the tabernacle (Exod. 24–31). He told Moses exactly how to build it, what materials to use, and how to offer the sacrifices and conduct the other acts of worship. God instituted tabernacle worship so that the people might maintain a holy walk with Him.

But while Moses was on the mountain working and praying for the people, what were the Israelites doing? They were growing impatient. Unbelief usually leads to impatience. If we are trusting the Lord, we will be willing to wait patiently for Him to lead when He chooses and as He chooses. Isaiah 28:16 tells us, "[He] that believeth shall not make haste" (KJV).

Not only were the people of Israel impatient, but they were ungrateful as well. When Moses didn't return right away, they replaced him with Aaron. What Moses had taught them was quickly swept aside in their desire to have their own way. Moses had left Aaron in charge while he was gone (see Exod. 24:14), but Aaron proved to be a weak leader who yielded to the wishes of the majority. When they asked him to build them an idol, he quickly complied, even though he knew it was wrong. Later, when Moses confronted Aaron with his sin, Aaron made excuses and blamed it on the people and even on the furnace, saying, "You know how prone these people are to evil. They said to me, 'Make us gods who will go before us.' . . . Then they gave me the gold, and I threw it into the fire, and out came this calf!" (32:22–24).

Moses became angry at the people because he realized that their sin was a sin of unbelief and rebellion against God. They had replaced Moses with Aaron; they had replaced God with a golden calf. Then they replaced holy living with idolatrous, immoral worship. Idolatry and immorality usually go together. Behind the people's wish for a golden idol was their secret desire to get back to Egypt. They didn't believe God when He promised to give them the Promised Land as their inheritance. They looked at the desert around them and longed to go back to the security they had known in Egypt, forgetting completely about the suffering and slavery they had experienced there.

They not only rebelled against God, they also rejected the leadership of Moses. Acts 7:39–41 tells us, "But our fathers refused to obey him [Moses]. Instead, they rejected him and in their hearts turned back to Egypt. They told Aaron, 'Make us gods who will go before us. As for this fellow Moses who led us out of Egypt—we don't know what has happened to him!' That was the time they made an idol in the form of a calf." Notice especially the statement "in their hearts turned back to Egypt" (v. 39). While the Israelites had been taken out of Egypt, Egypt had not been taken out of them. They were still looking back instead of looking forward to the Promised Land.

Exodus 32:6 tells us that the people rose early in the morning to have this idolatrous feast. It's amazing how people who are too tired to get up early for prayer or Bible study can rise at the crack of dawn for some other activity. The Israelites also gladly contributed their gold to build this idol. People are willing to pay for entertainment and sin, while begrudging what little they give for the Lord's work.

Three Philosophies of Life

In Exodus 32 we see three philosophies of life. Some, like the Israelites, believe in doing only what is easy and enjoyable. They live by the motto "If it feels good, do it." Then there are those like Aaron, who do what is popular. They believe that morality is based solely on what is accepted by the majority of society at that time. And finally we have the faithful few, like Moses, who do what is right, no matter what the cost. Their lives are not based on outward circumstances or on the opinions of others but solely on the Word of Truth.

We need more leaders like Moses today. Moses was not concerned about his own pleasure or popularity; he cared only about the glory of the Lord. He was a man of courage. He confronted an entire nation with their sin. He told his own brother, "You have sinned." But Moses was also a great man of compassion who returned to the Lord on the mountain and begged Him to forgive the people. If the Lord wouldn't forgive Israel's sins, then Moses was willing to be punished in their place (see 32:32). The apostle Paul had the same kind of compassion for the Jewish people. "I have great sorrow and unceasing anguish in my heart," he wrote. "For I could wish that I myself were cursed and cut off from Christ for the sake of my brothers, those of my own race, the people of Israel" (Rom. 9:2–3). Paul was willing to forfeit his own salvation in order to see others come to know the Lord.

When we consider the sin of the Israelites, we can see that Moses' anger was indeed justified and was within the will of God. Unfortunately, not all of us today display this kind of holy anger. We've become so tolerant of sin that we no longer weep or become concerned when we see how people openly defy the Law of God. My prayer is that God will help us, like Moses, to have a holy anger that comes from a broken heart, the kind of attitude that is willing to make any sacrifice to bring glory to God.

3

David
ANGRY AT OTHER PEOPLE'S SINS

It's always easier to find fault with others and to get angry at their sins while we ignore our own sins. But if we want to serve Christ with a clean heart, we must see our own sins first and seek God's cleansing and forgiveness. If we don't honestly deal with our own sins, God may have to discipline us, and that isn't a pleasant experience (see 1 Cor. 11:27–32). The Lord knows how to bring us to our knees in repentance, and no person in the Bible illustrates this truth better than King David. That account is given in 2 Samuel 12.

When we think of King David, a number of different images come to mind. We think of David the shepherd, faithfully caring for his father's sheep, or perhaps defeating the giant Goliath. We remember David the soldier who courageously fought the battles of the Lord. We also give thanks for David the singer who gave to us a wealth of beautiful songs in the Book of Psalms.

Unfortunately, when we think of David the shepherd, the soldier, and the singer, we can't help but remember David the sinner who committed adultery by taking Uriah's wife, Bathsheba. In an effort to cover up his sin, David arranged to have his loyal soldier Uriah murdered on the battlefield (see 2 Sam. 11). For at least a year, David covered up his sins from the people, but he couldn't hide his sins from God. "But the thing David had done displeased the LORD" (v. 27), and when God is displeased, He begins to act.

The Lord sent Nathan the prophet to David to deal with him about his sins of adultery, murder, and deception. Nathan didn't have an easy task. The king had been known to have a quick temper, and he exercised sovereign power in the land. If David refused Nathan's message, he could have the prophet banished from the land or even killed. No, Nathan didn't have an easy task before him, but he obeyed the command of the Lord.

The Lord helped Nathan handle the situation with compassion and skill. He knew that the king had a childlike spirit, so he treated David like a disobedient and stubborn child. He told David a story, and God used that story to break David's heart. Nathan first drew a picture for David, then turned that picture into a mirror so David could see himself, and then made the mirror a window through which David could see the Lord and seek forgiveness. Let's consider this threefold approach used by Nathan and see how it applies to our lives today.

The Picture

In dealing with sin in our lives, the first thing God does is bring the sin out into the open, for the Bible tells us, "He who conceals his sins does not prosper, but whoever confesses and renounces them finds mercy" (Prov. 28:13). David had been covering his sins for about a year, and so Nathan first showed David a picture designed to touch his heart and to remind him of his unconfessed sin. Here's the story Nathan told.

34

"There were two men in a certain town, one rich and the other poor. The rich man had a very large number of sheep and cattle, but the poor man had nothing except one little ewe lamb he had bought. He raised it, and it grew up with him and his children. It shared his food, drank from his cup and even slept in his arms. It was like a daughter to him.

"Now a traveler came to the rich man, but the rich man refrained from taking one of his own sheep or cattle to prepare a meal for the traveler who had come to him. Instead, he took the ewe lamb that belonged to the poor man and prepared it for the one who had come to him."

David burned with anger against the man and said to Nathan, "As surely as the LORD lives, the man who did this deserves to die! He must pay for that lamb four times over, because he did such a thing and had no pity." Then Nathan said to David, "You are the man!"

2 Samuel 12:1–7

Nathan's story deeply touched David's emotions, not only because it painted a picture of extreme cruelty and greed but also because it reminded him of his own past. David had been a shepherd and he understood the emotional ties that bind a shepherd to his sheep. David knew what it meant to be poor and also what it meant to be rich. As he listened to the story, in his imagination David looked at the picture Nathan painted, and he learned three important truths.

How David sinned. At first, David didn't see the connection between Nathan's story and his own life, but the meaning of the story is obvious. David was the rich man, and Uriah was the poor man with the much-loved ewe lamb, which represented Bathsheba. The traveler in the story pictures temptation. Temptation came to David's heart like a traveler knocking on the door, and instead of turning the traveler away, David invited him in and entertained him. Like Cain, David had a dangerous enemy at the door, and he should never have opened the door (see Gen. 4:6–7).

David made his first mistake when he left the battlefield and returned to Jerusalem alone. The Bible commands us to put on the whole armor of God, but it says nothing about taking it off and setting it aside (see Eph. 6:10ff). One night he took a walk on the roof of the palace and looking down saw his neighbor's wife bathing. At that moment temptation ("the traveler") came knocking at the door. Rather than locking the door and turning away, David chose to entertain his visitor. Soon, David gave into temptation and sent for Bathsheba, who obeyed the king's orders and came, and David lay with her (see 2 Sam. 11:1–4). The traveler became a friend, then a guest, and then the master of the house. One sin led to another, and soon David was being controlled by sin.

Temptation often comes to our door without warning and disguised as a traveler that won't stay long. If we open the door of our imagination and our heart to this traveler, he will come in as a guest. The longer we entertain the traveler, the faster the guest will become a friend and we become "comfortable" with the possibility of sinning. Suddenly, the friend becomes our master and temptation leads to sin. The important lesson here is simply: Don't open the door!

Why David sinned. He sinned because he forgot the goodness of God. The Lord had been good and generous to David, and Nathan reminded the king of what the Lord had done for him. God had saved David from Saul's deadly spear. He had made David king and had given him wealth, power, many wives and children, and a famous name. If all this had not been enough, the Lord would have given him much more (see 2 Sam. 12:7–8). David was the rich man in Nathan's story, and instead of stealing the poor man's lamb (Uriah's wife), he should have said, "God has been good to me. I have plenty. I don't need to rob somebody else." But instead, David robbed Uriah of his wife's loyalty and purity, and then he even robbed Uriah of his life.

Because David forgot the goodness of God, he refused to repent of his sin, for it's the goodness of God that leads us to repentance (see Rom. 2:4). After the Prodigal Son had squandered his inheritance and was living in poverty, he remembered the goodness of his father and it softened his hard heart. He said, "How many of my father's hired men have food to spare, and here I am starving to death!" (Luke 15:17). He repented of his sin and went home, where he was forgiven and restored.

When David saw Uriah's wife, he should have said, "Yes, this woman is very beautiful and desirable, but I won't allow myself to desire her. I have a loyal family and a good home. I have so many wonderful blessings. I don't need anything else. God has given me all that I need." Perhaps we can't be blamed for seeing a beautiful woman, but we can be blamed for the second look and for feeding the imagination because of that second look. Dwelling on the goodness of God and the blessings He has given us is one of the best ways to fight temptation.

The Devil baits his hook and says, "Don't you know that the Lord is holding out on you? If God really loved you, He would give you what I'm offering you." That's when we must stop and realize how good God has been to us. The writer James referred to this principle when he wrote: "[E]ach one is tempted when, by his own evil desire, he is dragged away and enticed. Then, after desire has conceived, it gives birth to sin; and sin, when it is full-grown, gives birth to death. Don't be deceived, my dear brothers. Every good and perfect gift is from above, coming down from the Father of the heavenly lights . . ." (James 1:14–17). Remembering the goodness of God will keep us from entertaining temptation and then rushing into sin.

What David's sin did to him. From the picture Nathan described we discover not only how David sinned (he entertained temptation) and why he sinned (he forgot the goodness of God) but also what the sin did to him. To begin with, David's sin blinded him. He saw somebody else's sins but not his own. "David burned with anger against the man . . ." (2 Sam. 12:5). Perhaps the king thought Nathan was bringing him an actual civil suit that he had to settle, because David didn't see himself in this story at all. Whenever we're hiding sin in our lives, it blinds us to ourselves and we find it easier to judge the sins of other people.

Because this is true, Christ's warning about judging others is even more important. He told us, "Do not judge, or you too will be judged. For in the same way you judge others, you will be judged, and with the measure you use, it will be measured to you" (Matt. 7:1–2). This is exactly what happened to David. He passed judgment on the man in Nathan's story, saying, "As surely as the LORD lives, the man who did this deserves to die. He must pay for that lamb four times over, because he did such a thing and had no pity" (2 Sam. 12:5–6). In passing judgment, David was only stating the punishment for stealing that had been instituted in the Law. "If a man steals an ox or a sheep and slaughters it or sells it, he must pay back five head of cattle for the ox and four sheep for the sheep" (Exod. 22:1). David knew the Law —but he also broke it.

However, David passed judgment on himself. Even though David deserved to die for committing adultery and murder, God spared David's life. However, David did ultimately pay fourfold. He couldn't give Bathsheba's husband back to her or restore Bathsheba's purity. But David was required to repay fourfold in the lives of his own children. First, the baby died that had been conceived in adultery (see 2 Sam. 12:15–19). Then David's son Amnon violated his sister Tamar and was subsequently murdered by his brother Absalom (see 13:1–32). Later, when Absalom tried to usurp the throne of his father, he was killed by David's captain, Joab (see 18:9–15). Then still another son, Adonijah, tried to take the throne from the chosen successor, Solomon, and was executed (see 1 Kings 2:13–25). How tragic that David saw his sins repeated in his own sons. What a price to pay!

The Mirror

As David listened to Nathan's story, he saw a picture of someone else's sin. But then Nathan turned the story around so that it became a mirror that reflected David's own face. No sooner did the king pass judgment on the rich man than Nathan confronted him with, "You are the man" (2 Sam. 12:7). What courage it took for the prophet to say this! Anyone who has tried to point out a person's sin to him knows how Nathan felt. Confronting fellow believers is one of the hardest tasks of the Christian life, but it is a necessary task. Because we frequently have difficulty recognizing problems in our own lives, we should welcome loving criticism from others. However, all too often we respond with anger and bitterness toward the person who is trying to help us.

David sinned grievously by committing adultery with Bathsheba and then having Uriah killed, but let's give him credit for taking an honest look at himself in the mirror, confessing his sins, and truly repenting. As David looked into this mirror, what did he see?

39

First, he saw a man who had experienced God's goodness. In pointing out David's sin to him, the prophet first reminded him of everything the Lord had done for him. God anointed David king over Israel, and delivered him out of the hand of Saul. God gave him wives and children as well as the house of Israel and Judah. "And if all this had been too little," said the Lord, "I would have given you even more" (v. 8). As David looked at himself in the mirror, he realized how ungrateful he had been for the tremendous blessings he had received from God.

The mirror also revealed to David a man who had despised God's Word. Even though David had been able to hide his sins from those around him, he could not hide them from God. Nathan reminded him vividly of his long-hidden sin, asking him, "Why did you despise the word of the LORD by doing what is evil in his eyes?" (v. 9). David knew the Ten Commandments, yet he chose to reject God's Word, and the Lord made it clear that despising His Word is the same as despising Him. The Lord told David, "Now, therefore, the sword will never depart from your house, because you despised me" (v. 10).

Not only did David see a man who had despised God's Word, but he also saw a man who had disgraced God's name. David had given occasion to God's enemies to show contempt toward the Lord (see v. 14). The Lord's name had been dragged down in disrepute because of what David had done. Israel's unbelieving neighbors saw how Israel's king behaved and assumed that the God of Israel was no different from their own gods. Because David had disgraced God's name, he would spend the rest of his life living in shame as well. The Lord told David that while he had taken Uriah's wife in secret, his neighbors would commit adultery with David's wives in public (see 2 Sam. 16:15–23). While David had used a devious plan to have Uriah killed, David's sons would be judged openly (see 2 Sam. 12:10–13).

David discovered how painful it is to examine ourselves closely in the mirror of God's Word (see James 1:23–25), but it's even more painful to lie about ourselves and avoid the truth. David saw a man who had experienced God's goodness and yet was ungrateful, a man who had despised God's Word and was unyielding, a man who had disgraced God's name and had hurt God's people. But without this examination, David could never have come to the place of repentance and forgiveness.

Like David, we need to take a good look at ourselves in the mirror of God's Word. All too often we just stop to glance at ourselves, merely hearing the Word but not applying it to our lives. Soon we begin to overlook our faults and sins and develop a self-righteous attitude about ourselves and a critical attitude toward others. Not only must we read the Word but we must also apply it daily to our lives. We must confess the sins that hinder our relationship with the Lord and disgrace His name.

How long has it been since you looked at yourself closely in this mirror?

The Window

When we examine ourselves closely in the mirror of God's Word, earnestly looking for any sin in our lives, this mirror eventually becomes a window through which we can see God and go to Him for forgiveness and healing. As David came face to face with his sin, he humbly and sorrowfully confessed, "I have sinned against the LORD" (2 Sam. 12:13). Nathan's response indicates that David's remorse over his sin and his subsequent confession were genuine, for Nathan told David that he had been forgiven. "The LORD has taken away your sin. You are not going to die" (v. 13).

What a wonderful demonstration of the grace of God! Adultery and murder were capital crimes according to Jewish law, and justice demanded that David be executed. However, because David expressed true repentance for his sins, God the Law-Giver became God the Redeemer and pardoned him. David experienced God's grace, but he also experienced God's government; for though God had forgiven his sin and had remitted the death penalty, David still had to suffer the consequences of pardoned sin. He spent the rest of his life reaping what he had sown. The little baby died. His son Absalom violated David's wives and Amnon raped David's daughter Tamar. Both Absalom and Adonijah rebelled against God and tried to take over the kingdom. David experienced the grief of having four sons die because of the sins he had committed.

The good things in life are paid for in advance, but we pay for our sins by the installment plan. For example, if you want to play good music, you spend time and money learning how to play an instrument. If you want to earn a good living, you invest time and energy mastering a job. If you want a beautiful garden, you plow and sow, weed and water. We pay for the good things of life in advance, but we pay for our sins on the installment plan, even the sins that God has already forgiven. While our sin may seem harmless at the time, we always pay for it later. Galatians 6:7–8 tells us, "Do not be deceived: God cannot be mocked. A man reaps what he sows. The one who sows to please his sinful nature, from that nature will reap destruction; the one who sows to please the Spirit, from the Spirit will reap eternal life."

When David looked at the picture that Nathan painted for him, his anger erupted at the sin of another person. But then that picture turned into a mirror, and David realized that he was looking at himself and his sin. Instead of becoming angry at Nathan or blaming others for his sin, David faced himself and his sin honestly and confessed it to God. As he did, this mirror became a window through which he saw the grace of God being extended to him. He heard words that brought peace and joy to his heart: "The LORD has taken away your sin. You are not going to die" (2 Sam. 12:13). One translation renders this passage: "The Lord has laid your sin on another." What a beautiful picture of what God has done for us through Jesus Christ! He has laid on Him the iniquity of us all (see Isa. 53:6). "If we confess our sins, he is faithful and just and will forgive us our sins and purify us from all unrighteousness" (1 John 1:9).

Is our anger at others a "cover up" for our own sins?

"He who conceals his sins does not prosper, but whoever confesses and renounces them finds mercy" (Prov. 28:13).

4

Elisha
ANGRY AT MISSED OPPORTUNITIES

What's the most important and most valuable thing in your church? Large financial resources? Modern facilities? A trained staff? While these are all good things to have, unless God's people have true faith and vision, they will miss great opportunities for ministry and growth.

The prophet Elisha became angry at the king of Israel because he didn't have faith and vision. He limited himself and, as a result, he also limited what God could do for him and for his people. The story is in 2 Kings 13.

> Now Elisha was suffering from the illness from which he died. Jehoash king of Israel went down to see him and wept over him. "My father! My father!" he cried. "The chariots and horsemen of Israel!"
>
> Elisha said, "Get a bow and some arrows," and he did so. "Take the bow in your hands," he said to the king of Israel. When he had taken it, Elisha put his hands on the king's hands.
>
> "Open the east window," he said, and he opened it. "Shoot!" Elisha said, and he shot. "The LORD's arrow of victory, the arrow of victory over Aram!" Elisha declared. "You will completely destroy the Arameans at Aphek."

Then he said, "Take the arrows," and the king took them. Elisha told him, "Strike the ground." He struck it three times and stopped. The man of God was angry with him and said, "You should have struck the ground five or six times; then you would have defeated Aram and completely destroyed it. But now you will defeat it only three times."

2 Kings 13:14–19

For years, Hazael, the king of Aram, had been attacking Israel and Judah. After Hazael had defeated Gath, he was on his way to attack Jerusalem when the king of Judah stripped the temple of its treasures and sent them to Hazael as a peace offering, along with some of his own treasures (see 12:17–18). Because the Lord was angry at the nation of Israel for their many sins, He allowed Hazael and his son Ben-hadad to oppress them (see 13:3). So, when Jehoash, king of Israel, heard that the prophet Elisha was dying, he became worried. He went to Elisha, hoping to receive some blessing before the prophet died. Elisha did indeed give Jehoash a blessing: The army of Israel would get the victory over Aram.

However, in saying this, Elisha was also testing the faith and vision of Jehoash, and he found him seriously lacking. King Jehoash was a man who limited himself. Because he didn't have the faith and vision to ask great things of God, he didn't receive all that God could have given him. When you examine this event in the life of King Jehoash, you discover that he suffered from four limitations. We need to be aware of these limitations so that we can avoid making the same mistakes in our lives, our churches, and our ministries.

A Limited Appreciation of God's Servant

King Jehoash didn't recognize and acknowledge what a great and godly man Elisha really was. Elisha was a man of great courage and faith, a man who had received special power from the Lord. He was successor to Elijah the prophet, and when Elijah was taken into heaven by a whirlwind, Elisha received a double portion of Elijah's spirit because he saw it happen (see 2 Kings 2:1–13).

God worked mightily through Elisha and gave him a long, fruitful ministry. Elisha ministered during the reigns of five different kings of Israel, and Scripture records twenty different miracles that Elisha performed, including one that he performed after he was dead and buried (see 13:20–21). God enabled him to part the Jordan River (2:14) and to purify polluted water (vv. 19–22). He multiplied the widow's oil so she could pay her bills and rescue her children from slavery (4:1–7). Elisha possessed power over disease and death. He healed Naaman of his leprosy (5:1–14) and raised a young boy from the dead (4:18–37). In addition, Elisha delivered a number of prophecies, including one that promised that Israel would defeat the Moabites (3:10–27). Indeed, Elisha was a man who was powerfully used by God. He was also a great man of prayer.

Knowing this, you would think that the kings of Israel would have sought Elisha's wisdom and help, but this was not the case. The kings consulted Elisha only in emergencies when they were in impossible situations and needed divine help (see 3:4–14). (That sounds like some of God's people today!) They weren't interested in learning the Word of the Lord or doing the will of the Lord. But when Elisha was about to die, King Jehoash showed up and wept by the prophet's deathbed, saying, "My father! My father! The chariots and horsemen of Israel!" (13:14).

Jehoash didn't recognize Elisha's role as the spiritual father of Israel until the prophet was about to die. Elisha had been caring for the people, helping them and teaching them the Word of God, but the king hadn't paid much attention. The prophet did everything a father does as he gave spiritual nourishment, protection, and guidance to the children of Israel. Yet, it appears that the king hadn't followed the prophet's leadership or appreciated his ministry until it was almost too late.

Isn't this what so often happens in our lives? We take our parents, grandparents, and other relatives and friends for granted, and then they're taken from us. Suddenly, they become very important to us! We wish we had listened more to them and learned from them. What opportunities we've wasted when the Word was preached and we didn't pay attention!

King Jehoash not only had ignored the spiritual leadership of Elisha, but he hadn't recognized what a key role Elisha played in Israel's military victories. Jehoash finally realized that, without Elisha's intercession before God, the nation would have suffered defeat long ago. Because of Elisha, the Lord gave deliverance to the people on many occasions. The king told the prophet that he was more important to the nation than all the chariots and horsemen of Israel. Elisha was a one-man army!

What is a church's greatest asset? It's not buildings, or budgets, or clever programs, but godly people who walk with the Lord, who know the truth of God, who know how to pray, and who have faith and vision. As Christians, we should desire to live in such a way that our contributions to our nation, our church, and our family will be missed after we are gone. Churches today need more one-man and one-woman armies like Elisha!

This final incident in the earthly ministry of Elisha also shows us that our work for the Lord is never finished until the moment we take our last breath. Even on his deathbed, the elderly prophet was still displaying the power of God. He prophesied Israel's defeat of Aram, telling the king to take the bow and arrows and to shoot an arrow out the window to the east. In Old Testament times, when you wanted to declare war on another nation, it was a common practice to shoot an arrow into the enemy's territory. Since Aram was located east of Israel, Elisha was demonstrating to Jehoash that the Lord would give them victory in their war with Aram. Not only did Elisha prophesy the victory, but he laid his hands on the king's hands and gave Jehoash the power and blessing of the Lord that would enable him to accomplish this victory.

We can learn another important lesson from Elisha. Even though he was dying, he was still thinking about others. He could have spent his time feeling sorry for himself, pondering why the Lord didn't take him home miraculously the way He took Elijah. Why did he have to endure pain and suffering? But Elisha understood that God has different plans for different people. So instead of questioning God or wallowing in self-pity and depression, Elisha spent his last days on earth thinking about others and serving the Lord. The prophet showed a genuine concern for the king and his nation. He was grieved over the constant conflict with the Arameans and wanted to do what he could to help. So once again, he allowed himself to be the instrument God used to proclaim His message of deliverance.

Elisha had been faithfully serving the Lord and the nation of Israel for about sixty years, yet Jehoash didn't recognize and appreciate this servant of God until it was almost too late. What about you? Have you told your pastor lately that you appreciate his ministry and that you pray for him daily? Have you told your aged relatives and friends that you love them and thank God for them? What about your children, your mate, your friends? Let's show appreciation to the people God uses in our lives and thank the Lord for them while we still have opportunity. They may be taken from us when we least expect it.

A Limited Understanding of God's Will

Not only did King Jehoash not appreciate the ministry of Elisha until it was too late, but he also had a limited understanding of God's will. Elisha's instructions and prophecy were clear. He told Jehoash to shoot an arrow out the window, signifying Israel's challenge to battle. Then the prophet instructed him to take the arrows and "strike the ground with them" (2 Kings 13:18). Jehoash obeyed, but he struck the ground only three times, revealing that he didn't really grasp God's plan. The arrows represented the victory that God was going to give the king. The number of times Jehoash struck the ground determined how many victories he would receive from the Lord.

The meaning of Elisha's prophecy should have been clear to Jehoash, but the king lacked spiritual discernment. He had a limited understanding of the will of God because he had a limited understanding of God Himself. It's a tragedy when Christians can't discern what God is doing in their lives. It's especially tragic when we face a crisis with no understanding of what God wants to accomplish. Moses is an example to us of a man who knew what God was doing because he was open to God's revelation. Psalm 103:7 tells us, "He [God] made known his ways to Moses, his deeds to the people of Israel." Because Moses had a close relationship with the Lord, he not only saw *what* the Lord was doing but he also knew *why* He was doing it. Moses understood God's will because he was directly involved in obeying it.

The children of Israel, on the other hand, were merely spectators. They saw the acts of God but didn't really understand the reasons behind them. Like Jehoash, they were limited in their understanding.

Unfortunately, too many believers today are armchair Christians. They sit back and watch God work without understanding His purposes. Why? Because they haven't learned enough about the Lord and His Word to understand His principles. They've failed to develop that intimate relationship with Him that leads to understanding His will and His ways of working. Therefore, they fall apart when a crisis comes and begin to accuse God of not caring about them.

How sad it is when we have a limited understanding of God's will. We need to pray constantly, "Teach me Thy will, O Lord." We must read and meditate on the Word of God in order to discover the mind of God. The apostle Paul knew the importance of knowing God's will. That's why he prayed "that the God of our Lord Jesus Christ, the glorious Father, may give you the Spirit of wisdom and revelation, so that you may know him better. I pray also that the eyes of your heart may be enlightened in order that you may know the hope to which he has called you, the riches of his glorious inheritance in the saints, and his incomparably great power for us who believe" (Eph. 1:17–19). Paul prayed that believers would understand what God had done, what He was doing, and what He would do in the future for those who trusted Him. It isn't enough just to know the will of God; we must also seek to understand it (see Eph. 5:17).

A Limited Faith in God's Power

King Jehoash had a limited appreciation of God's servant and a limited understanding of God's will. He went through the motions, but he didn't really know why he was doing it.

51

Jehoash had a third limitation that prevented him from using the opportunities presented to him: He had a limited faith in God's power.

Elisha had good reason to become angry at Jehoash. He had bluntly told the king exactly what was going to happen. The arrow the king shot was the arrow of the Lord's victory over Aram (see 2 Kings 13:17). However, Jehoash didn't claim the Lord's promise by faith. He underestimated the power of God. Elisha told Jehoash that if he had really believed God, he would have beaten the ground five or six times rather than only three. Therefore, Jehoash's victory was limited by his faith.

No doubt Elisha died a disappointed man. He had spent his life ministering to the children of Israel, trying to bring them back to God. When King Jehoash showed so little faith, Elisha may have wondered if the people had heard anything he had taught them. He may have asked, "Is there any faith left in Israel?" Jesus asked, "However, when the Son of Man comes, will he find faith on the earth?" (Luke 18:8).

God works in response to our faith. In healing two blind men, Jesus told them, "According to your faith will it be done to you" (Matt. 9:29). The kind of faith we have either releases God's power or limits God's power. When we have great faith, nothing is impossible (see 17:20). However, the Lord limits His work when unbelief is present (see 13:58). He leaves the choice up to us. He will only empower us to the degree that we want to be empowered.

A Limited Victory in God's Service

Because Jehoash had a limited understanding of God's will and a limited faith in God's power, he experienced a limited victory in God's service. In 2 Kings 13:25 we are told, "Then Jehoash son of Jehoahaz recaptured from Ben-hadad son of

Hazael the towns he had taken in battle from his father Jehoahaz. Three times Jehoash defeated him, and so he recovered the Israelite towns." Why was Jehoash successful only three times? Because he struck the ground with the arrows only three times. The Lord gave him what he expected.

We find an important principle at work here. Public victories are based on private victories. Before David met Goliath on the battlefield and killed him in full view of both armies, he had already killed a lion and a bear while herding his sheep alone. Before Jesus suffered public death on the cross, He had already surrendered to the Father's will in the Garden of Gethsemane. Our outward actions are a reflection of our inward attitudes. If we aren't walking with God privately, then our public service will be limited and ineffectual.

Even though we have God's promise of complete victory through Jesus Christ (see 1 Cor. 15:57), many Christians are experiencing only partial victories because their spiritual lives are sadly lacking in faith. They're not meeting God privately each day to commune with Him. They're not acting by faith and claiming the promises of God. Yet, they blame the Lord for their failures when they are really at fault. This is the tragedy of lost opportunity!

Because King Jehoash failed privately, he limited himself publicly. He could have defeated the Arameans completely, but he chose to limit God's power because he didn't discern God's will. As a result, the whole nation of Israel suffered from Syrian oppression in the years to come.

Jehoash had four serious limitations in his life that caused him to miss the opportunities God wanted to give him for victory. He had a limited appreciation of God's servant, Elisha. He apparently had taken Elisha for granted until he thought the prophet was about to die. Only then did he

53

realize how important Elisha was to the nation. Likewise, Jehoash had limited understanding of God's will. Because the king's relationship with the Lord was not what it should have been, he didn't understand God's plan for defeating the Arameans. He merely went through the motions of obeying the Lord without knowing why he was doing it. This led to a limited faith in God's power. Jehoash underestimated what the Lord could do for him. Because he didn't have the faith to claim God's promises, he experienced a limited victory. As a result, both he and the nation of Israel suffered.

The same principles apply to our lives and our service today. When we limit the Lord, we're not the only ones who suffer. Churches grow weak when believers live on partial victories, and families don't mature spiritually when parents live with spiritual limitations. Elisha was justified in being angry at Jehoash for missing a God-given opportunity to be a conqueror. We should be angry at ourselves whenever we try to limit God. The Lord wants to give us great victories in His service, both for our blessing and for His glory. There's no limit to what we can do in the will of God when we trust Him completely. The Lord is "able to do immeasurably more than all we ask or imagine, according to his power that is at work within us" (Eph. 3:20). Nothing is impossible for God to do when we believe and obey. Let's not limit Him by our ignorance and unbelief. Let's claim the promises of God and win His victories for His glory.

5

Uzziah

ANGRY BECAUSE HE GOT CAUGHT

Anger can be a wonderful tool in the hands of God, if the anger is holy and justified. However, selfish, sinful anger can be a terrible weapon in the hands of the Devil. Frequently, selfish anger leads us to commit sins that hurt others. Cain's anger led to jealousy and eventually to murder. However, even if our rage does not seriously harm others, sinful anger still hurts us and might even destroy us. In fact, the person who is angry is always hurt far more than those with whom he is angry.

We see this fact graphically illustrated in the life of King Uzziah. During the days of the Old Testament monarchy, the word of the king was law. The king held the power of life and death because he was God's deputy on earth and was responsible for enforcing God's Law. Therefore, above all else, the people wanted to avoid making the king angry. They knew that the results could be deadly! In fact, God's Word warned them against enraging the king. Proverbs 16:14 states, "A king's wrath is a messenger of death, but a wise man will appease it." Proverbs 20:2 adds, "A king's wrath is like the roar of a lion; he who angers him forfeits his life."

This placed a great responsibility not only on the people but also on the king. He had to make sure that his anger was righteous and not selfish and proud.

King Uzziah manifested unholy anger and hurt himself and his rule. Second Chronicles 26 records this sad story of a good king gone bad, and the unhappy consequences.

His fame spread far and wide, for he was greatly helped until he became powerful.

But after Uzziah became powerful, his pride led to his downfall. He was unfaithful to the LORD his God, and entered the temple of the LORD to burn incense on the altar of incense. Azariah the priest with eighty other courageous priests of the LORD followed him in. They confronted him and said, "It is not right for you, Uzziah, to burn incense to the LORD. That is for the priests, the descendants of Aaron, who have been consecrated to burn incense. Leave the sanctuary, for you have been unfaithful; and you will not be honored by the LORD God."

Uzziah, who had a censer in his hand ready to burn incense, became angry. While he was raging at the priests in their presence before the incense altar in the LORD's temple, leprosy broke out on his forehead. When Azariah the chief priest and all the other priests looked at him, they saw that he had leprosy on his forehead, so they hurried him out. Indeed, he himself was eager to leave, because the LORD had afflicted him.

King Uzziah had leprosy until the day he died. He lived in a separate house—leprous, and excluded from the temple of the LORD. Jotham his son had charge of the palace and governed the people of the land.

verses 15–21

In the account of Uzziah's reign in 2 Kings 15 and 2 Chronicles 26, you discover that he was a highly successful and popular king who had faithfully followed the Lord for many years. Yet, here we find him blatantly sinning. He of all people should have known that only the priests could offer incense in the Holy Place of the temple. However, when the priests confronted him with his sin, King Uzziah didn't repent but instead lost his temper. In fact, the Hebrew word for *anger* used in this passage literally means "to boil up, to storm." This word was often used in describing a raging sea. This was no mild anger; Uzziah was furious at the priests and having a temper tantrum in the house of God. What would cause this king, who had been so faithful, to become angry as he did? In looking closer at this incident, we find at the heart of his disobedience and anger a number of other sins, sins that every Christian can fall prey to unless we are very careful.

An Ungrateful Heart

Behind Uzziah's anger lurked the sin of an ungrateful heart. The Lord had greatly blessed King Uzziah and given him a long and prosperous reign. Apart from this particular sin, Uzziah has been remembered throughout history as a wise and faithful ruler. The Bible tells us, "He did what was right in the eyes of the LORD . . ." (2 Chron. 26:4). God had blessed Uzziah in remarkable ways because he truly sought the Lord's will for his life. "He sought God during the days of Zechariah, who instructed him in the fear of God" (v. 5). Zechariah (not to be confused with the one who wrote the Book of Zechariah) was one of the godly prophets of that time. Unlike many of the kings before him, Uzziah sought Zechariah's friendship and help in understanding the will of the Lord. Uzziah listened eagerly to the prophet's teachings from the Word of God and obeyed them to the best of his ability.

It also appears that Uzziah had a godly mother who may have instilled in him the desire to please God. Her name, Jecoliah, means "Jehovah will enable." Since Uzziah was

57

only 16 years old when he ascended the throne of his father, Amaziah, his mother no doubt had a great influence on him and on his reign during those early years. Through the influence of his mother and his friend Zechariah, Uzziah sought to follow the Lord. As a result, "God gave him success" (v. 5).

Uzziah had a successful army and won victory after victory. King Uzziah had 307,500 soldiers and 2,600 officers at his command (see vv. 12–13). He also had an abundant supply of equipment—shields, spears, helmets, armor, bows, and slingshots (see v. 14). In addition, his men had invented specialized equipment similar to catapults for guarding the walls and towers of the cities and for attacking the enemy (see v. 15). Not since the time of David had the nation of Judah had such a reputation for military strength. The Lord helped them defeat both the Philistines and the Arabians (see vv. 6–7). The Ammonites feared the Jewish army so much that they brought peace offerings to Uzziah. No wonder Uzziah's fame spread throughout the nations and even reached as far as Egypt (see v. 8).

King Uzziah also enjoyed success and prosperity at home. He initiated a number of building programs and improved the water supply. He was also a successful farmer who deeply loved working the soil. He had huge herds of cattle and many farms and vineyards (see vv. 9–10).

King Uzziah was not only a man who was greatly blessed by God, he was a man whose life seemed to be balanced. He knew how to battle but he also knew how to build. He was a man of peace as well as a man of war. He was a wise and just ruler whose name was honored by his friends and enemies alike. And Uzziah knew that the source of his success was God alone. Yet, with each new victory, Uzziah became less grateful and more proud. He began to want something more.

Sometimes the stronger and more successful we become, the greater is the temptation to get proud and start taking the credit. We forget that our strength and prosperity come from God, and we begin to rely on our own strength and to desire more and more glory. When that happens, we need to remember the Lord's warning: "Pride goes before destruction, a haughty spirit before a fall" (Prov. 16:18).

An Unholy Ambition

One of the first symptoms of spiritual decay is that we lose our gratitude and forget that God made us what we are and helped us succeed in what we did. Cultivating an ungrateful heart can lead us to commit a second sin—cultivating an unholy ambition.

Ambition is a good thing if it's motivated by God's will, obedient to God's Word, and leads to God's glory. The Christian should be ambitious to grow in the Lord and to seek additional opportunities for serving Him. Too many believers become comfortable and satisfied in their work for the Lord. They rest on their past accomplishments rather than continuing to do all they can for Him. However, when our ambition is not motivated by God's will and by obedience to God's Word, then it is unholy and destructive. God had given Uzziah every blessing. He was a wealthy and powerful king. Yet, he was not satisfied just to be a king; he wanted to be a priest as well. He ignored God's laws concerning the priesthood and attempted to assert his own authority and get what he wanted.

The Bible records many examples of people who exercised unholy ambition. Nadab and Abihu, the sons of Aaron the high priest, wanted to have more authority in the tabernacle and they brought strange fire to God's altar. As a result, God sent fire from heaven to consume them (see Lev. 10:1–2). In Numbers 16, we read about Dathan and Abiram, the sons of Eliab, who defied the authority of Moses. God's punishment of their unholy ambition was swift. The Lord caused the ground to open up and swallow these men and their followers (see vv. 31–33). Even Miriam, the sister of Moses, complained after Moses had been made the highest leader of the nation, because she felt she had as much authority as he did. She said, "Has the LORD spoken only through Moses? Hasn't he also spoken through us?" (12:2). As a result of her unholy desire for power, God struck Miriam with leprosy.

In the New Testament, the classic example of unholy ambition is a man named Diotrephes. In 3 John, verse 9, we read: "I wrote to the church, but Diotrephes, who loves to be first, will have nothing to do with us." Because of his selfish desire for power and authority in his church, Diotrephes rejected the apostle John and anyone who associated with him. Not only did Diotrephes refuse to receive John and the other leaders when they came to visit, but he disciplined any church member who welcomed these men. Diotrephes was practicing what he thought was separation; however, it was merely isolation. John condemned this kind of attitude: "So if I come, I will call attention to what he is doing, gossiping maliciously about us. Not satisfied with that, he refuses to welcome the brothers. He also stops those who want to do so and puts them out of the church" (v. 10).

We must be careful not to have unholy ambition. This is what turned the angel Lucifer into Satan. He said to himself, "I will make myself like the Most High" (Isa. 14:14). Whenever people begin looking for more authority, power, and importance, and seek things that are outside the will of God, they will only create trouble for themselves and for others. We need to seek God's will for our lives and to make it our sole ambition to please Him. King Uzziah was blessed greatly when he served the Lord alone, but then he began running ahead of God, wanting authority that didn't belong to him. As a result, Uzziah lost what authority and honor he had and became a leper.

An Unyielded Will

Because King Uzziah forgot the blessings he had received from God and was blinded by his unholy ambition, he didn't yield his will to the Lord. Uzziah was familiar with the laws that governed the Jewish priesthood. God's Word had made it clear to Aaron: "But only you and your sons may serve as priests in connection with everything at the altar and inside the curtain. I am giving you the service of the priesthood as a gift. Anyone else who comes near the sanctuary must be put to death" (Num. 18:7). Even though King Uzziah knew God's Law, he ignored it and did as he pleased. He had become so proud that he believed God would make an exception for him.

But when it came to the priesthood, God didn't make exceptions to His commandments. Like Uzziah, King Saul thought he was above God's Law and assumed the office of priest, offering a sacrifice for the people. Saul's punishment was swift and final: His kingdom was taken away from him and from his descendants (see 1 Sam. 13:8–14). In the Old Testament, we find only one example of a king who was also a priest—Melchizedek (see Gen. 14:18). His name means "king of righteousness," and he was the king of Salem, which means "peace." He was called the "priest of God Most High" (v. 18). But Melchizedek ruled before God instituted the

61

Levitical priesthood, and he was given as a picture of Jesus Christ, who is both King and Priest.

Jesus Christ our Lord is "a high priest forever, in the order of Melchizedek" (see Heb. 6:20; chaps. 7–10). He is also the King of kings (1 Tim. 6:15). Jesus is the king of righteousness and of peace. Righteousness and peace have been joined together in the Lord Jesus Christ because of Calvary. And because of what Christ has done for us, each believer is also a king and a priest. "To him who loves us and has freed us from our sins by his blood, and has made us to be a kingdom and priests to serve his God and Father . . ." (Rev. 1:5–6). Through Jesus Christ, every true believer belongs to a royal priesthood (see 1 Peter 2:9).

King Uzziah wanted to start a royal priesthood, but this wasn't the will of God. Even when he was confronted with his sin, he still did not repent. Azariah and eighty other priests came to Uzziah in the temple and warned him not to sin by offering the incense. They begged him to leave quickly. But instead of repenting, the king became enraged at them (see 2 Chron. 26:19). Because Uzziah refused to yield his will to the Lord, he brought God's judgment upon himself.

An Unhappy Life

The life of King Uzziah is a perfect illustration of God's warning: "So, if you think you are standing firm, be careful that you don't fall" (1 Cor. 10:12). Uzziah had faithfully served God for most of his life. He had brought glory to the Lord and had been greatly blessed as a result. But then he allowed an ungrateful heart, an unholy ambition, and an unyielded will to rob him of these blessings. His life from that time forward was filled with unhappiness and misery. Uzziah spent his declining years alone, as a leper. What a great tragedy it is when a faithful believer, who has served God for many years, sins against the Lord and spends his or her final years in shame and loneliness.

The results of Uzziah's sin were threefold. First, he lost his health. Because Uzziah refused to repent, he brought God's judgment on himself. He was immediately stricken with leprosy. According to the Law, anyone who interfered in the priest's ministry or even entered the areas of the temple reserved for the priests was to be put to death. However, the Lord, in His mercy, chose to spare Uzziah's life. He instead cut Uzziah off from the people and forced him to spend the rest of his life in isolation as a leper.

The second result was a natural outgrowth of the first. Because of his leprosy, he lost his throne. Technically, Uzziah was still the king. However, because lepers were not allowed to be near people, Uzziah had to turn control of his kingdom over to his son Jotham (see 2 Chron. 26:21).

Not only was Uzziah cut off from his people and his position, but he also lost his privilege of going to the temple. Uzziah had disobeyed the will of God by trying to penetrate into the very heart of the temple. As a result, he was cut off from every area of the house of the Lord (see v. 21).

King Uzziah had to learn the hard way what happens when we don't learn to control ambition and anger. When confronted with his sin, Uzziah displayed anger at the wrong people and for the wrong reasons. Instead of becoming angry at himself and at his sin, he lashed out at those who were trying to bring him back to the will of God. His pride and temper kept him from seeking God's forgiveness. If he had only repented, he could have avoided much unhappiness and heartache.

Uzziah had won many battles and conquered many cities, but he never learned to control the kingdom within. He didn't understand the truth of Proverbs 16:32: "Better a patient man than a warrior, a man who controls his temper than one who takes a city." Learning to control anger and selfish ambition will help us enjoy success in the Christian life. "A patient man has great understanding, but a quick-tempered man displays folly" (Prov. 14:29).

How do we gain control over a quick temper? By remembering God's goodness to us and expressing gratitude for everything He has given us. By directing our ambitions toward His purposes and His glory, and by yielding our will to His will. Only then can we experience the inner strength and peace that will enable us to control the rage within us.

No matter how much blessing we have enjoyed or service we have rendered to the Lord, we must be on guard. "Watch out that you do not lose what you have worked for, but that you may be rewarded fully" (2 John 8). May God help us all to end well!

6

Jonah
AN ANGRY PREACHER

Many people have the idea that anger is always a sign of strength. On the contrary, it can be an evidence of weakness and fear. In the Old Testament, we meet an angry preacher. By the world's standards, this man had a successful ministry. He preached only one sermon and a whole city repented and turned to the Lord. However, in God's eyes, he was really a failure. That preacher, of course, was Jonah. He allowed his anger and animosity toward the Ninevites to destroy the joy and blessings of his ministry.

The story of Jonah is a familiar one. If the Book of Jonah had ended with chapter 3, verse 10, Jonah would have looked very successful. Even though he had rebelled against God's call in the beginning, he experienced a miraculous answer to prayer while inside the belly of a great fish. Not only was his life spared, but he saw a tremendous awakening take place in Nineveh as a result of his preaching. But though it appeared that Jonah's attitude toward the Ninevites had changed, in his heart he still harbored anger and resentment toward them and also toward the Lord.

It's possible to be in the place of the Lord's appointment and still have a sinful heart—one that is hard, angry, and rebellious toward God. Jonah knew how to pray and how to preach, and his theology was grounded solidly in God's Word, yet he still became angry when he didn't get his own way with the Lord.

> But Jonah was greatly displeased and became angry. He prayed to the LORD, "O LORD, is this not what I said when I was still at home? That is why I was so quick to flee to Tarshish. I knew that you are a gracious and compassionate God, slow to anger and abounding in love, a God who relents from sending calamity."
>
> Jonah 4:1–2

When God called him to go to Nineveh, Jonah realized that the Lord would spare the people if they repented, and Jonah wanted the Ninevites to be destroyed. They were a wicked people and the enemies of the Israelites. Jonah ran away from the Lord rather than preach to a people he hated. Finally, after Jonah learned that he couldn't successfully run from God, he reluctantly went to Nineveh; and there Jonah's worst fears were realized. The people did repent and turn to the Lord, and God spared the city. Like a child who doesn't get what he wants, Jonah began to pout and to feel sorry for himself. "Now, O LORD, take away my life, for it is better for me to die than to live" (v. 3).

The Lord graciously responded to Jonah's anger and self-pity by saying, "Have you any right to be angry?" (v. 4). The Lord forced Jonah to be reasonable, to focus on his reasons for being angry. If Jonah had been honest with himself, he would have seen that his anger was unjustified. He should have been happy for the salvation of the Ninevites and excited that God allowed him to have a part in their repentance. But the prophet wasn't ready to repent of his anger just yet.

> Jonah went out and sat down at a place east of the city. There he made himself a shelter, sat in its shade and waited

> to see what would happen to the city. Then the LORD God provided a vine and made it grow up over Jonah to give shade for his head to ease his discomfort, and Jonah was very happy about the vine.
>
> verses 5–6

In the back of his mind, Jonah was still hoping that God would destroy the city. So, just in case, he left the city and built himself a shelter nearby so he could watch what happened. Despite Jonah's repeated disobedience and rebellion, the Lord still cared for his needs. He caused a large plant to grow immediately, providing shade for Jonah. Just a few short hours before, Jonah had been exceedingly displeased (v. 1). Now he was exceedingly glad for the Lord's provision of this plant (v. 6). Jonah was a man who was controlled by his emotions, not by his devotion to the Lord. The Lord also had another reason for providing this plant for Jonah. He used it to teach the prophet an important lesson about unjustified anger.

> But at dawn the next day God provided a worm, which chewed the vine so that it withered. When the sun rose, God provided a scorching east wind, and the sun blazed on Jonah's head so that he grew faint. He wanted to die, and said, "It would be better for me to die than to live."
>
> verses 7–8

Jonah's reaction reveals to us an important truth about anger: Anger, self-pity, and depression often go together. People who are controlled by anger often experience periods of depression and self-pity and don't even realize that their anger is the cause of their depression.

While Jonah was sitting there feeling sorry for himself, the Lord spoke to him again, driving home the point of this object lesson.

But God said to Jonah, "Do you have a right to be angry about the vine?"

"I do," he said. "I am angry enough to die."

But the LORD said, "You have been concerned about this vine, though you did not tend it or make it grow. It sprang up overnight and died overnight. But Nineveh has more than a hundred and twenty thousand people who cannot tell their right hand from their left, and many cattle as well. Should I not be concerned about that great city?"

verses 9–11

The Lord told Jonah, "If you can have compassion on a plant that you didn't even plant or tend, why can't I have compassion on the people of Nineveh, whom I created?" Unfortunately, the story ends here. We don't know how Jonah responded to the Lord. We can only hope that if there were a verse 12, it would read: And Jonah repented and said, "O Lord, forgive me for my anger. I will now go back into the city and finish my job for your glory."

What is your personal response to the experience of Jonah? Do you sympathize with his dilemma and say, "I agree with you, Jonah. Those Ninevites were wicked people and they deserved to die. Like you, I'm angry, too. I'm angry that God is allowing wicked people to continue doing whatever they want." Most of us don't agree with Jonah and we wouldn't want to be like him, but often we respond to the unsaved in much the same way as he did. Like Jonah, we can be overjoyed at some small, insignificant honor or material possession we receive, yet we can't feel happy when our enemy is converted or feel sad at the sin in our life. Anger shifts the focus of our priorities from what God wants to what we want.

This is why it is so dangerous for Christians to allow selfish anger to control their hearts. When we're angry, we tend to convince ourselves that our anger is righteous indignation when we're really expressing godless, selfish, worldly anger. When we give in to this kind of anger, the Lord can't bless us or use us to reach others.

The Reason for His Anger

Why did Jonah become angry at God for sparing the Ninevites? What was Jonah's reason for becoming angry? Actually, the answer is very simple: incomplete surrender to God. In order to use us, the Lord must have control of every aspect of our being—our body, mind, will, and heart. We must yield ourselves completely to Him. We can hold nothing back.

Throughout the Book of Jonah we find the prophet holding out on God, but gradually the Lord gained control of the various aspects of Jonah's life. In chapter 1, God communicated to Jonah's mind, telling him, "Go to the great city of Nineveh and preach against it . . ." (v. 2). But, at this point, the Lord didn't have control of the rest of Jonah. Jonah's will resisted God and the prophet refused to go to Nineveh. His heart agreed totally with this rebellion, and the two caused his body to run away from God. But try as he might, Jonah could not rid his mind of God's words to him.

In chapter 2, God used circumstances to bring Jonah to the place where he would surrender his will to Him. As Jonah lay in the belly of a great fish, he cried out to God: "But I, with a song of thanksgiving, will sacrifice to you. What I have vowed I will make good" (v. 9). Once the Lord had Jonah's will, He rescued his body from the belly of the great fish. In chapter 3, you see Jonah's mind and will directing his body to go to Nineveh.

Even though Jonah obeyed the Lord and preached in Nineveh, he was still not controlled by God, for his heart was not in his ministry. It seems incredible that Jonah could preach one of the greatest revival sermons in Old Testament history, yet hate the people to whom he was preaching! What a tragic illustration of the truth stated in 1 Corinthians 13:1: "If I speak in the tongues of men and of angels, but have not love, I am only a resounding gong or a clanging cymbal." We can be among the greatest preachers in history, but if we don't have a sincere love for the people we're preaching to, our words will be empty and meaningless.

However, the results of Jonah's preaching teaches us another important lesson about our service: God will use His Word even if His servant is not all that he should be. Even though Jonah's heart was not in his ministry, the Lord blessed His Word anyway, and the people repented despite Jonah's efforts to hinder them. It is possible for the Lord to bless a ministry without blessing its minister. When our hearts are not right with God, we will miss the many wonderful benefits that can come from our service to the Lord. However, God can and does accomplish His work in spite of our weaknesses.

Without love, any sacrifice we make or service we perform is worthless: "If I have the gift of prophecy and can fathom all mysteries and all knowledge, and if I have a faith that can move mountains, but have not love, I am nothing. If I give all I possess to the poor and surrender my body to the flames, but have not love, I gain nothing" (vv. 2–3). Why is ministry worthless to servants who have no love? Because God can't fully bless the person who is doing the ministering. Others may get blessing from the Word, but the preacher is left empty.

Even though Jonah had not given his heart to God and to the people, the Lord still chose to use Jonah's ministry to lead the people to repentance. He did so because of His great love for the people and His compassion for the innocent children of Nineveh. The Lord's final words to Jonah are interesting because they reveal the Lord's compassion for all the people in the city, including the little children and even the cattle! It seems likely that the one hundred twenty thousand persons that God was referring to in Jonah 4:11 were young children who had not yet reached the age of accountability and couldn't discern right from wrong.

If this interpretation is correct, then we can see how large the city of Nineveh actually was. It was described as a "great city" (v. 11), and when you add parents to the number of little children, as well as older children and adults without children, the population of this city could have been close to a million. Many commentators estimate that the population of Nineveh was at least six hundred thousand. In this passage, the Lord was trying to make Jonah see how many innocent people would have died if He had destroyed the entire city because of the wickedness of the adults.

To show Jonah the depth of His compassion, the Lord even expressed His concern for the animals. He told Jonah, in effect, "If all these people die in judgment, who will take care of the animals?" Jonah didn't have this kind of pity. He thought primarily about himself.

Jonah was unwilling to surrender himself completely to God because his attitudes were all wrong. Jonah had a wrong attitude toward God's will. He thought God's will was something you could accept or reject, not something to be obeyed without question. So, when the Lord called Jonah to go to Nineveh, the prophet made up his mind to ignore God's will and to do as he pleased. Jonah also had a wrong attitude toward prayer. He believed in praying only when he was in trouble and needed the Lord's help. To Jonah, prayer was simply a magic charm to get what he wanted. Likewise, Jonah had the wrong attitude toward obedience.

He obeyed the Lord because he had to, not because he wanted to. His service was motivated by a sense of duty and of fear rather than from a genuine love for the Lord and for His people. Finally, Jonah had a wrong attitude toward lost souls. He didn't love unbelievers, and his lack of love revealed itself in his anger toward the Ninevites and toward God, for not destroying them.

The Results of His Anger

No matter what reasons you may have for becoming angry—whether holy or unholy—you will reap consequences. If your anger is righteous and just, then the results will be constructive. However, if your anger is rooted in selfishness and an incomplete surrender to God, as Jonah's anger was, then it will only lead to tearing down your Christian life. You always lose when you harbor anger against God and against other people.

Even if we are justified in our anger against a brother, nurturing that anger or seeking revenge against the person not only is wrong but also often hurts us far more than it hurts others. We need to leave judgment and punishment to God. "Do not take revenge, my friends, but leave room for God's wrath, for it is written: 'It is mine to avenge; I will repay,' says the Lord" (Rom. 12:19).

When you look at the life of Jonah, you discover only one person who really suffered from his anger—Jonah himself. While his fellow passengers on the ship suffered temporary peril because of his disobedience (see Jonah 1:4–15), and while Jonah's anger may have hurt some people in Nineveh, in the end only Jonah suffered real loss.

First, he lost his testimony. When Jonah saw that the people had repented, he left the city. God had opened the door for ministry for him in Nineveh, and Jonah should have been seizing the opportunity to pray with the people and teach them about the true God. But, instead, you see Jonah leaving his place of ministry and sitting outside the city, thinking only of himself. Even if Jonah did repent after his encounter with God and go back into the city, he no doubt found it nearly impossible to teach effectively. The people would have found it hard to trust him after what they had seen.

Not only did Jonah lose his testimony, but he also lost his love. Jonah allowed anger and hatred to destroy his love for God and for other people. His anger caused him to isolate himself from the fellowship he needed to build him up. As he sat alone, brooding over his anger, he became more and more despondent. Self-pity and a sense of hopelessness soon set in, and Jonah wanted to die. He cried out, "Now, O LORD, take away my life, for it is better for me to die than to live" (4:3). Whenever we allow anger to replace love in our hearts, we start to feel hopeless and lonely. Anger tears you apart inside, while love builds you up.

In addition, Jonah lost God's guidance. The Lord had a special plan for Nineveh, and Jonah was the key to that plan. However, the prophet refused God's guidance and abandoned the place of God's blessing, and the Lord had to discipline His servant. Then Jonah wanted to die rather than complete the Lord's work in Nineveh. He lost God's guidance because he was too wrapped up in himself to be concerned about others.

He also lost God's Word. Once Jonah left the city, we don't find God giving him any new revelation. When the Lord spoke, it was only to rebuke Jonah for his anger. Likewise, Jonah lost power in prayer. He was praying only for himself. He showed no concern for the needs of others.

Because Jonah no longer wanted God's guidance, he lost his sense of values. I've seen this happen when people begin to be controlled by anger. Anger produces incomplete obedience to God. This, in turn, causes our values to become distorted. Little things take on giant proportions, and what is really significant seems of small value. Because of his disobedience and anger, Jonah became self-centered and valued only what would benefit him. Jonah rejoiced over the simple plant that God sent to shade him, yet he refused to celebrate with the people of Nineveh over the revival they had experienced. Likewise, when the gourd died, Jonah regretted it, but he felt no sorrow for the lost souls in Nineveh. Why? Because he had forgotten what it was like to be lost. He had forgotten how the Lord had saved him from the belly of the fish.

In the life of Jonah, we see the consequences of a broken relationship with the Lord. Without the Word of God and prayer to guide him, Jonah lost his faith and joy. He wanted the Lord to destroy the city and even to destroy him. He didn't have the faith to understand why God would spare it. Jonah's service in Nineveh wasn't motivated by love and faith but by anger and fear. He was serving the Lord with madness, not gladness (see Ps. 100:2). Like Jonah, some Christian workers don't serve the Lord out of gladness and joy, nor do they minister because they love people. How unlike our Lord Jesus Christ!

The Remedy for His Anger

Instead of rejoicing with the people of Nineveh about God's deliverance, Jonah became angry. Why? Because he had not surrendered himself completely to God. He had the wrong attitude toward God's will and toward the people of

Nineveh. As a result, Jonah lost his fellowship with the Lord. He no longer had God's Word and prayer to guide him. His faith, love, and joy were gone. And his testimony to the people was destroyed—all because of unjustified anger.

What's the remedy for this kind of unrighteous anger? A good dose of honesty and humility! Jonah first needed to be honest with God and with himself. Throughout the Book of Jonah, we find the prophet arguing with God. When the Lord called Jonah and told him to go to Nineveh, Jonah turned and ran the other way. Everything in the Book of Jonah obeys God except Jonah—the wind, the sea, the worm, the vine, the great fish, even the lost people in Nineveh! When God didn't destroy Nineveh, Jonah's response was, "I knew this would happen! These people deserve to die, so why don't you destroy them?" (see Jonah 4:2).

Isn't this what usually happens when we allow anger to rule us? Instead of admitting that we were wrong, we become defensive and argumentative. Like Jonah, we justify our anger and self-pity, saying, "I have good reason to be angry" (see v. 9). So, the first step in overcoming our anger is to admit to ourselves and to God that we are angry without just cause.

Honesty is just the first step. We must also have humility. Jonah should have fallen on his face before God and said, "O Lord, I've learned my lesson. I disobeyed you before and after I came to Nineveh. Forgive me. Remove this anger and hatred from my heart. Help me to do Your will." Forgiveness and healing cannot take place until we willingly surrender ourselves completely to God. If we try to rid ourselves of the anger and malice inside us, we'll fail miserably. Only God by His Spirit can remove the hatred that lurks deep within us and replace it with a spirit of love and forgiveness. "God has poured out his love into our hearts by the Holy Spirit, whom he has given us" (Rom. 5:5). This kind of love is stronger than anger. When we allow ourselves to be God's channel of love to others, then we experience His love in a deeper way in our own lives. When we are being loved, there is no room for anger.

The remedy for anger is to become like the God whom we represent. Jonah knew what kind of God he served, but he wasn't willing to give Him the complete surrender and obedience that was required. "I knew that you are a gracious and compassionate God, slow to anger and abounding in love . . ." (Jonah 4:2). The Holy Spirit can replace our anger with God's love, mercy, patience, and kindness when we surrender our total being—body, mind, heart, and will.

"They will know we are Christians by our love."

7

An Angry Army

We have all had people become angry with us at one time
or another, but imagine having one hundred thousand men
all angry at you at the same time! Imagine also that they are
soldiers skilled in the use of weapons. You can see the
dilemma you would be facing. What would you do?

One man in the Bible found himself in that situation—
Amaziah, the king of Judah. We read in 2 Chronicles 25:5–10:

> Amaziah called the people of Judah together and assigned
> them according to their families to commanders of thou-
> sands and commanders of hundreds for all Judah and Ben-
> jamin. Then he mustered those twenty years old or more and
> found that there were three hundred thousand men ready
> for military service, able to handle the spear and shield. He
> also hired a hundred thousand fighting men from Israel for
> a hundred talents of silver.
>
> But a man of God came to him and said, "O king, these
> troops from Israel must not march with you, for the LORD
> is not with Israel—not with any of the people of Ephraim.
> Even if you go and fight courageously in battle, God will
> overthrow you before the enemy, for God has the power to
> help or to overthrow."
>
> Amaziah asked the man of God, "But what about the hun-
> dred talents I paid for these Israelite troops?"

The man of God replied, "The LORD can give you much more than that."

So Amaziah dismissed the troops who had come to him from Ephraim and sent them home. They were furious with Judah and left for home in a great rage.

King Amaziah made a grave mistake in hiring the Israelite soldiers. He didn't seek the Lord's will in the matter and as a result created problems for himself and for the kingdom of Judah. He angered an entire army and was forced to deal with the consequences of their anger. Like Amaziah, sometimes we run ahead of the Lord and create problem situations for ourselves, and then we try to take the easy way out of our predicament. But there are no shortcuts to dealing with anger and the difficulties it creates. As we consider this angry army, three questions come to mind. The answers to these questions give us God's instructions for dealing with our anger and with those who are angry at us.

Who Was the Target of Their Anger?

The army of Israel was angry at the kingdom of Judah in general and at Amaziah, the king of Judah, in particular. As you will recall, the Israelite nation divided following the death of Solomon and the ascension of his son Rehoboam to the throne. The tribes of Benjamin and Judah formed the Southern Kingdom called Judah. They continued the house and lineage of David and, for the most part, remained faithful to God. The other ten tribes comprised the Northern Kingdom of Israel, also called Ephraim. Unlike Judah, the nation of Israel fell into idolatry and formed their own religion. Before Israel was conquered by Assyria, the nation was marked by great wickedness and unfaithfulness to the Lord. Because of

Israel's wickedness and unbelief, Judah and Israel were in almost constant conflict with each other.

Why would Amaziah appeal to his idolatrous enemy for help in fighting this war, especially when he knew that God didn't approve of Israel? We find help in answering this question from 2 Chronicles 25:2: "He [Amaziah] did what was right in the eyes of the LORD, but not wholeheartedly." Amaziah was a half-hearted follower of the Lord. The king's obedience to God was not everything it should have been. His faith often wavered, and he frequently tried to do things his own way and not the Lord's way.

God wants total obedience from His children, for He knows that anything less will only cause us grief. James 1:8 tells us that a double-minded man is "unstable in all he does." The Bible warns us against being double-minded but encourages us to be wholehearted in our devotion to the Lord. In Matthew 6:19–21, Jesus told us, "Do not store up for yourselves treasures on earth, where moth and rust destroy, and where thieves break in and steal. But store up for yourselves treasures in heaven, where moth and rust do not destroy, and where thieves do not break in and steal. For where your treasure is, there your heart will be also." When the heart is divided between devotion to Christ and a love of worldly possessions, the world will always win out in the end. That's why it is important for us to commit everything we have to Him.

Likewise, the Lord doesn't want servants whose minds are divided. In Matthew 6:22–23, Jesus added, "The eye is the lamp of the body. If your eyes are good, your whole body will be full of light. But if your eyes are bad, your whole body will be full of darkness. If then the light within you is darkness, how great is that darkness!" In this passage, Jesus tells us that outlook determines our outcome and that we can't successfully look in two directions at the same time. If we try to keep our eyes both on Jesus and on the world, we'll develop double vision, and double vision ultimately produces spiritual blindness. People with divided minds become ineffective because it is impossible for them to give their complete attention to pleasing the Lord in all things.

But Jesus also warned us against being double-willed: "No one can serve two masters. Either he will hate the one and love the other, or he will be devoted to the one and despise the other. You cannot serve both God and Money" (v. 24). Many people today have divided loyalties, trying to serve the Lord and the world at the same time. But this never works and we must make a choice. Choosing to follow Christ involves a total commitment—our whole heart, mind, and will. We can't be half-hearted in our Christian life and enjoy the blessing of God.

Amaziah's mind was divided, looking both to the Lord and to the unfaithful Israelites for help. Instead of wholeheartedly trusting God for the victory, he put his faith in the numerical strength that money could buy. Amaziah had four hundred thousand soldiers with which to fight the Edomites, but with the Lord's help, he could have won with far fewer men and saved his money. But Amaziah put his faith in numbers instead of in God, so he hired one hundred thousand mercenaries from the enemy, Israel, paying them a hundred talents of silver. Like so many people, Amaziah relied on human resources to solve his problems and not on the Lord.

Amaziah's response to the rebuke from the man of God reveals what was in his heart: He was more concerned about money than he was about the glory of God. "But what about the hundred talents I paid for these Israelite troops?" (2 Chron. 25:9). The king wasn't concerned about pleasing God but rather how much it would cost him to please God.

The money was obviously more important to him than obedience. He would rather keep his money and lose God's blessing.

When we start counting the cost of obedience, we're heading for trouble. Jesus made this fact perfectly clear.

> As they were walking along the road, a man said to him, "I will follow you wherever you go."
>
> Jesus replied, "Foxes have holes and birds of the air have nests, but the Son of Man has nowhere to lay his head."
>
> He said to another man, "Follow me."
>
> But the man replied, "Lord, first let me go and bury my father."
>
> Jesus said to him, "Let the dead bury their own dead, but you go and proclaim the kingdom of God."
>
> Still another said, "I will follow you, Lord; but first let me go back and say good-by to my family."
>
> Jesus replied, "No one who puts his hand to the plow and looks back is fit for service in the kingdom of God."
>
> Luke 9:57–62

These men missed the blessing of following Jesus and sharing in His wonderful ministry because they weren't willing to pay the price of obedience.

This incident in Amaziah's life also shows us the cost of disobedience. He knew that he should not have hired the soldiers from Israel, but he wanted victory more than obedience. As a result, he suffered tremendous financial loss, not to mention even greater spiritual loss. Scholars disagree on exactly how much a talent of silver was worth in that day, but many estimate that Amaziah's one hundred talents of silver would have been worth more than two million dollars. One study Bible lists the amount at $2,184,000. Amaziah couldn't retrieve that money since he had already paid the soldiers. By sending them home, he didn't even receive the return from his investment. You may be thinking to yourself, How could someone be so foolish? Amaziah should have known that disobedience doesn't pay, that no amount of money can cover our sins! Yet how much have we spent to cover our disobedience or to get our own way?

Amaziah made a mistake by hiring this army. When he was confronted with his sin, he should have simply sent the army home and forgotten about the money. He did reluctantly dismiss the soldiers, but he still worried about losing his money instead of trusting God to supply his needs. The man of God told the king, "The LORD can give you much more than that" (2 Chron. 25:9).

Yes, we must pay a price for our disobedience, but we must not dwell on our mistakes. Once we have confessed our sins, we need to forget about them and trust God to help us in the future. Obedience and disobedience both require an investment on our part. But the Lord's dividends for obedience far outweigh the temporary benefits of our disobedience.

What Were the Reasons for Their Anger?

It seems strange that the Israelite soldiers became angry at Amaziah for sending them home. After all, they had received their pay without having to earn it, and they never faced the dangers of the battle. You would think that they would have been glad to escape with their lives and their wages. Why were they angry? I believe that a number of factors were involved.

The first reason for their anger was pride. They had been embarrassed publicly, and nobody likes to be embarrassed. When the king dismissed them, no doubt the rumors started to fly. The people may have been saying, "Why aren't they living up to their agreement? What kind of soldiers are they anyway? I heard that the man of God told the king to send them home because the Lord was not with Israel. They would have only caused us trouble. After all, Israel is our enemy, you know. They would have probably turned traitor in the middle of the battle." When our pride is injured, our first response is to lash back in anger. We become defensive and vengeful. As we will see, this is exactly how these Israelite soldiers responded (see 2 Chron. 25:13).

A second reason for their anger was selfishness. These men were mercenaries, and mercenaries fight simply to earn money. They weren't concerned at all about Judah or its holy cause. If the Edomites had offered the Israelites two hundred talents of silver, they would have deserted Amaziah and his army in an instant and fought for the other side. Even though they had each received a large sum of money for those days, they wanted more. For a soldier, one of the benefits of war was being able to take the spoils after the battle. While he had to give the king a portion of whatever he took, he could still make quite a bit of money from plundering. Thus, these soldiers became angry because they were being denied the spoils of war; so they went out and plundered Judah instead (see v. 13). They robbed their own relatives to satisfy their selfishness and pride.

It's frightening what people will do just to make money! Everywhere we look today, we find people whose only goal in life is to become as rich as they can. They will do whatever it takes to make a profit, reasoning that the end justifies the means. They will step on other people in order to reach the top. They have no ethical standards, but while they're making a living, they're not making a life. Often those who reach the top find nothing satisfying waiting there for them. This is why we see so many miserable, lonely, and hopeless people in our world today. They haven't yet learned that only Christ can give them true riches and satisfaction. Jesus gives us eternal life and abundant life.

It's also likely that national pride was involved in the anger of these soldiers. These men were Israelites, and their country had been at war with Judah for many years. For this reason, they didn't like the Judeans. Once again, pride entered in—pride for their country. While true patriotism is an excellent thing, when pride takes over, nationalism takes over and can become destructive. We begin to think that we're better than others and that others must do what we want done. If they don't, we have a right to "defend our honor" and destroy others if necessary. This kind of pride can take on many forms: pride of country, state, or city, of our family, our school, or even of an athletic team. When someone appears to be threatening this excessive pride, we become angry and defensive. Satan can use this kind of attitude to create problems for us and for others.

A fourth reason for their anger was probably disgust. These soldiers had made a long trip to Judah for nothing. They had come prepared for battle and now had to take everything back home. No doubt they were annoyed and disgusted at the inconvenience. Instead of becoming angry, however, they should have seen what a blessing it was to be in the nation of Judah. They should have been thankful to be in a country where the people worshiped the true God. If these soldiers had really been smart, they would have wanted to stay and serve the Lord. But their selfishness and pride kept them from seeing their opportunity.

Isn't it remarkable and tragic how we can become angry over the smallest matters? The slightest hurt or injustice, the simplest selfish desire, the smallest inconvenience will sometimes send us into a fit of rage. Stop and evaluate your own anger. How many times have one of these causes—

pride, selfishness, or disgust—been at the root? The first step in overcoming anger is to identify the object of our anger and the reasons behind it. Then we need to admit that we are foolish for becoming angry for no valid reason and make an effort to dispel these angry thoughts before they cause problems.

What Were the Consequences of Their Anger?

Unjustified anger almost always has grave consequences, both for us and for others. What were the consequences of this army's anger? Second Chronicles 25:13 tells us. "Meanwhile the troops that Amaziah had sent back and had not allowed to take part in the war raided Judean towns from Samaria to Beth Horon. They killed three thousand people and carried off great quantities of plunder." Amaziah and his army had gone to fight the Edomites, leaving the villages in Judah unprotected. Since the Israelite soldiers couldn't punish Amaziah, they vented their anger on the innocent people of Judah. They ravaged the villages and took whatever they wanted, killing three thousand men, women, and children in the process.

After soundly defeating the Edomites, Amaziah and his army returned to find the destruction left by the Israelite army. The king was enraged, and no doubt embarrassed, by what the Israelite soldiers had done. Once again pride and nationalism entered in. Amaziah, who was feeling proud and strong after his victory, decided to go to war with Israel in order to avenge himself and his country (see vv. 17–19).

Once the cycle of anger starts, it is hard to stop. Seeking revenge only leads to retaliation from the other side, and soon the anger is out of control. When this happens, innocent people are caught in the crossfire. If we can't vent our anger on those who caused our rage, we frequently vent it on others, usually on anyone in our path. This is what the Israelite army did. Since they couldn't punish Amaziah, they took out their anger on his people instead.

In Amaziah, we see the danger of anger that is motivated by sin and pride. Even after the Lord corrected Amaziah for his faithlessness in hiring the Israelite army, he continued to ignore the Lord. God gave the king a great victory over Edom, and how did he repay Him? By replacing the Lord with idols from the country he had just conquered! Imagine worshiping the gods of the defeated enemy! "When Amaziah returned from slaughtering the Edomites, he brought back the gods of the people of Seir [Edom]. He set them up as his own gods, bowed down to them and burned sacrifices to them. The anger of the LORD burned against Amaziah . . ." (vv. 14–15). God sent a prophet to Amaziah to confront him with his sin and to pronounce judgment on him (vv. 15–16), but once again, Amaziah allowed anger to blind him to his sin. Instead of confessing his guilt, Amaziah became angry with the prophet and with God.

Amaziah's foolish anger blinded him to his own sin, and his pride blinded him to the consequences of his anger. The prophet told Amaziah, "I know that God has determined to destroy you, because you have done this and have not listened to my counsel" (v. 16). But Amaziah became proud. He thought he could win the battle without the Lord's help. So he ignored the prophet's warning and challenged Joash, the king of Israel, to meet him on the battlefield. Even Joash tried to warn Amaziah, saying, "You say to yourself that you have defeated Edom, and now you are arrogant and proud. But stay at home! Why ask for trouble and cause your own downfall and that of Judah also?" (v. 19). But Joash's warning only served to anger Amaziah even further. He attacked Joash and his army and was soundly defeated on the battlefield; and, once again, innocent men were killed because of his foolishness.

When we use anger and pride as a cover for sin, it always leads to problems. Proverbs 16:18 tells us, "Pride goes before destruction, and a haughty spirit before a fall." Proverbs 18:12 adds, "Before his downfall a man's heart is proud, but humility comes before honor." If Amaziah had only humbled himself and confessed his sins to God instead of becoming angry, he could have saved himself and the nation a great deal of heartache and loss. But he became his own worst enemy. Joash and his army broke down the walls of Jerusalem and took the gold, the silver, and the holy vessels from the temples. They also took Amaziah's personal treasures (see 2 Chron. 25:21–24). Amaziah wasn't killed in the battle, but his sins continued to haunt him. He was later assassinated by his own people (see vv. 27–28). Amaziah lost his wealth, his honor, and eventually his life because of his pride, selfishness, and anger.

Anger is like a small hole in a dike. It doesn't appear to be much of a problem at first. However, if the hole isn't plugged up quickly, the water will gradually enlarge the hole until the dam breaks and then people are faced with a raging flood. This is why Proverbs 17:14 warns us, "Starting a quarrel is like breaching a dam; so drop the matter before a dispute breaks out."

When we become angry, we must resolve it immediately. Anger that continues to burn within us soon becomes an uncontrollable fire that destroys us and those we love. Proverbs 26:21 sates, "As charcoal to embers and as wood to fire, so is a quarrelsome man for kindling strife." When we become angry, we add fuel to the fire. What otherwise might have been a minor problem soon grows beyond control when encouraged by anger.

The key to dealing with anger is self-control, which only the Holy Spirit can produce in us. When anger arises, we must take an honest look at ourselves to determine the source of that anger. If it's the result of pride, selfishness, or some other sin, we should humbly confess our sins to God. He will then fill us with the love that we need to control the anger within us. "But the fruit of the Spirit is love, joy, peace, patience, kindness, goodness, faithfulness, gentleness and self-control" (Gal. 5:22–23).

8

An Angry Congregation

Have you ever been angry at a preacher? Were you ever in a congregation that was so angry it got up and escorted the preacher out and then tried to kill him? While it is unlikely that any congregation in the United States would physically harm their minister, believers do become angry at the pastor and other church members and frequently attack them verbally. However, missionaries in other countries sometimes are abused or even killed by the people they have come to serve.

The Bible speaks of a number of prophets and preachers who gave their lives because they proclaimed God's message of salvation. Stephen is just one example. His sermon, recorded in Acts 7, so angered those listening that they immediately took him out and stoned him (see vv. 54–60).

Likewise, the greatest minister who ever preached also suffered this kind of abuse. What is even more ironic is the fact that He was in His own hometown preaching among His friends and neighbors. That man, of course, was Jesus Christ. "All the people in the synagogue were furious when they heard this. They got up, drove him out of the town, and took him to the brow of the hill on which the town was built, in order to throw him down the cliff. But he walked right through the crowd and went on his way" (Luke 4:28–30).

What would cause the people from our Lord's hometown to turn against Him that way? What did He say that made them so angry? And why do Christians today become angry at fellow believers? Let's attend that synagogue service in Nazareth and watch the congregation as it moves from one experience to another. By discovering the dynamic at work in that situation, we can learn some of the causes of anger in the Body of Christ today and find ways to deal with it.

They Were Assembled

In Luke 4:16 we see the congregation in Nazareth assembled in the synagogue for their weekly time of prayer and instruction. However, this was no ordinary Sabbath service, for Jesus had decided to join them: "He went to Nazareth, where he had been brought up, and on the Sabbath day he went into the synagogue, as was his custom. And he stood up to read" (4:16).

In that day, the weekly synagogue service was very important to the spiritual life of the Jewish people. The word *synagogue* means "gathering together." In the Old Testament, the tabernacle, and later the temple, were the primary places of worship. When the people of Israel were taken into captivity and then scattered throughout the nations, they could no longer come to the temple regularly to worship and offer sacrifices. They developed local synagogues where they could meet for the reading and expounding of the Scriptures and for prayer. The purpose of the synagogue was not so much worship as it was instruction. Unlike the temple, the synagogue was open to all the people, but only the men could participate in the service. Children were permitted to come to the synagogue from the age of five or six and were required to attend the services once they reached the age of sixteen.

While the intent and purpose of the synagogue had been good in the beginning, by the time of Christ we find that the Jewish religion had decayed tremendously. The Pharisees and other religious leaders had added so many interpretations to the Law that the Jewish faith had become a religion of works rather than faith in the living God. So many rules and regulations existed that the people couldn't possibly obey them all. Many people went to the synagogue out of a sense of obligation rather than from a real desire to learn God's Holy Word.

Yet we find Jesus attending the synagogue services regularly. We can think of reasons why He might have chosen not to meet there each Sabbath. He certainly had no need for learning the Law, and the religious leaders of the nation were sinful and rebellious. The synagogue services lacked real meaning and personal application. Christ had come to show the people a better way and to lead them back to God. To us, it would have seemed more logical for Jesus to reject the institutions and practices of the day and to work apart from the local congregations. However, He often chose to work in the synagogue, despite its flaws and problems.

Sometimes I hear people say, "The church is full of hypocrites and sinners. The sermons and classes are boring. Besides, I don't need to go to church to be a good Christian. I can worship God just as well at home, maybe better." However, God's Word tells us: "And let us consider how we may spur one another on toward love and good deeds. Let us not give up meeting together, as some are in the habit of doing, but let us encourage one another—and all the more

as you see the Day approaching" (Heb. 10:24–25). Not only
has the Lord commanded Christians to meet together regularly, but He also set the example for us. We need the fellowship and worship that the local church provides, despite
its flaws and problems.

They Were Attentive

Once Jesus stood up and began to read the assigned
Scripture for the day, the congregation immediately became
attentive. We find this same kind of response wherever Jesus
went. He always spoke with such authority and power that
the people couldn't help but listen. The people's attention
was focused on two things: the reading of God's Word and
the preaching of God's Word.

> The scroll of the prophet Isaiah was handed to him.
> Unrolling it, he found the place where it is written:
>   "The Spirit of the Lord is on me,
>   because he has anointed me
>   to preach good news to the poor.
>   He has sent me to proclaim freedom for the prisoners
>   and recovery of sight for the blind,
>   to release the oppressed,
>   to proclaim the year of the Lord's favor."
>
> Luke 4:17–19

Before delivering His message to the people, Jesus
began by reading from Isaiah 61. Christ's example here
shows us the importance of reading God's Word in public. First Timothy 4:13 exhorts God's people to maintain
the public reading of the Word of God in their assemblies.
When the early believers broke away from the synagogue,
they took this practice with them. The public reading of

the Scriptures was a part of every service in the early church, and it should be an important part of our worship today.

Unfortunately, many evangelical churches today have abandoned this practice. I'm amazed at how many people who claim to defend and to preach the Word of God don't encourage the public reading of the Scriptures. Often the sermon text is the only passage that is read during a service. We need to have a balanced reading of the Old Testament, the Gospels, and the Epistles. The Word of God is the spiritual food of the church and must not be neglected.

It was said of Dr. G. Campbell Morgan, the British expositor, that people learned more from his public reading of the Scriptures than they did from the sermons of other preachers. Why was this true? First and foremost was the fact that he was reading God's Word. The Scriptures have the power to transform lives. God's Word never returns to Him void (see Isa. 55:11). However, Dr. Morgan was especially successful because he carefully prepared for his public readings of the Word. Before he stood to read, he always studied the passage thoroughly. Many churches don't see results from their public Bible readings because they don't have this kind of preparation. I've attended services where someone has been asked at the last minute to stand to read the Word of God. This is wrong. Before God's Word is read publicly in any worship service, the readers should prepare their hearts and minds through personal study of the passage and prayer. That way they will be able to read the Scriptures with meaning and power.

Not only should we be faithful in the public reading of God's Word, but this incident in the life of Christ also shows us the importance of being attentive to the preaching of the Word. When Jesus had finished reading from the Book of Isaiah, He rolled up the scroll, gave it back to the minister in charge, and sat down. Everybody in the synagogue was watching him with anticipation, and they heard Him make a remarkable statement: "Today this scripture is fulfilled in your hearing" (Luke 4:21). Jesus then proceeded to teach them the meaning of Isaiah's prophecy.

In stating that He was the fulfillment of this prophecy, Jesus was claiming a great deal. The Greek word translated *sent* in verse 18 is *apostello*, a word meaning "to be sent forth on a mission and with a commission." It was used to refer to those who had received a special commission from God Himself. From this word we get the word *apostle*. This particular passage in Isaiah 61 was a messianic prophecy. Thus, Jesus was boldly proclaiming, "I am this promised Messiah." In fact, verse 18 is a revelation of the Trinity: "The Spirit [Holy Spirit] of the Lord [the Father] is on me [the Son]."

Furthermore, Christ said He had come "to proclaim the year of the Lord's favor" (Luke 4:19). This was a direct reference to the Year of Jubilee. When God gave the Law to the Israelites, He told them to set aside every fiftieth year as a year of rest and restoration (see Lev. 25). There was to be no sowing or reaping that year so the soil could rest. Also, property that had been sold to pay a debt was to be returned to the original owners or their heirs. Likewise, those who had sold themselves into slavery to pay a debt were to be released. Many celebrations were held during this time. The Year of Jubilee was a year of redemption and rejoicing. Thus, Jesus was saying, in effect, "I am proclaiming a spiritual Year of Jubilee. I have come to bring redemption and rejoicing." According to Isaiah's prophecy, five kinds of people would be helped by Messiah when he came. In each we discover both a literal and a spiritual fulfillment.

First, Jesus said that the Spirit of the Lord had anointed Him to preach the gospel to the poor (see Luke 4:18). Unlike many of the religious leaders of His day, Jesus frequently ministered to the poor in Palestine. He provided for their physical needs and their spiritual needs. But even more important, Jesus came to help the "poor in spirit" (Matt. 5:3). Who is poorer than a lost sinner? No one is rich enough to purchase his redemption. Only Christ can save us. We are all spiritually bankrupt until by faith we draw on His grace.

Jesus also said that He came to heal the brokenhearted and to give sight to the blind (v. 18). Of course, He did heal many people of blindness and other illnesses and often gave words of encouragement to the lonely and depressed. But greater still is the spiritual healing that we receive when we give Him all the pieces of our broken hearts and lives. He came to help the spiritually blind and to open their eyes to the truth of God's Word.

Finally, Jesus announced that He had come to "release the oppressed" (v. 18). During His ministry Jesus freed many people from sickness, demons, and death. There is no greater freedom than to be released from the terrible bondage of sin and Satan.

What a message of hope Christ has given us! He offers freedom and help to everyone, no matter how bankrupt, brokenhearted, bound, blind, or bruised they may be. The good news of the gospel is that we don't have to stay the way we are. Jesus Christ can transform our lives when we give ourselves to Him.

They Were Astonished

As Jesus spoke to the people, they listened attentively. However, their reaction reveals that His message had not changed their hearts and minds: "All spoke well of him and were amazed at the gracious words that came from his lips.

'Isn't this Joseph's son?' they asked" (Luke 4:22). The people were astonished at what Jesus told them; however, not in the way that we might imagine. They were shocked and surprised that He would make such claims about Himself, because they didn't believe that He really was the Messiah.

Why did they have too much trouble accepting what Jesus told them? Because they thought they knew Him when really they were ignorant of who He was and what he came to do. After all, Jesus had grown up among them in Nazareth. They knew He was the foster son of Joseph the carpenter and that he Himself was a skilled carpenter. Even though they had probably recognized that there was something different about this young man, they could never pinpoint exactly what it was. However, even when Jesus told them what made Him so special, they refused to believe it. Christ simply didn't fit their conception of God's promised Messiah.

The people were astonished not only at what Jesus claimed to be but also at what He claimed they were. They said to themselves, "What does this have to do with us? Do we look blind or bruised? Are we being held captive? We certainly aren't poor and destitute. Why do we need to trust Jesus? We have the religion of our fathers." Because they couldn't accept who Jesus was or admit their own spiritual need, the people didn't apply God's Word to themselves.

They Were Alarmed

However, there was more to come, and the rest of our Lord's message alarmed them. The point was all too clear.

> Jesus said to them, "Surely you will quote this proverb to me: 'Physician, heal yourself! Do here in your home town what we have heard that you did in Capernaum.'

"I tell you the truth," he continued, "no prophet is accepted in his home town. I assure you that there were many widows in Israel in Elijah's time, when the sky was shut for three and a half years and there was a severe famine throughout the land. Yet Elijah was not sent to any of them, but to a widow in Zarephath in the region of Sidon. And there were many in Israel with leprosy in the time of Elisha the prophet, yet not one of them was cleansed—only Naaman the Syrian."

Luke 4:23–27

When the people heard this, they became alarmed. Why? Because they realized that Jesus was no ordinary rabbi. Other teachers would simply reiterate what those before them had said. They would exalt the people of Israel and talk about its great future. But Jesus spoke with power and authority, and He knew exactly what the people were thinking and feeling. He exposed their unbelief. Jesus told them, in effect, "I know what you are thinking. You're saying to yourselves, 'If you really are the Messiah, then show us what you can do. Perform a miracle, and then we'll believe you.' However, miracles alone will never change your hearts. I know you won't accept me. A prophet is never accepted in his own country."

Jesus then exposed their pride. He reached back into Jewish history and gave them two examples of prophets who had ministered to people whom the Jews had rejected (see vv. 25–27). When we examine these examples closely, we can understand the impact Jesus' words made on these people. The people that were helped by Elijah and Elisha were not Jews, but Gentiles! The widow of Zarephath was a Sidonian and Naaman was a Syrian. Neither one was a Jew or even a Jewish proselyte.

This becomes significant when we remember how the Jews felt about themselves and about the Gentiles. They took

97

great pride in the fact that Israel was God's chosen people, and they looked down on anyone who wasn't a Jew. It was inconceivable to them that God would do something for the Gentiles. And here was Jesus, reminding these Jews in Nazareth that God had not only helped two Gentiles but had given them something that the Jews themselves had rejected. The meaning was all too clear. "If you continue to reject me, I will offer God's grace and salvation to the Gentiles." And that's exactly what happened.

Nothing smashes the pride of sinful man like the sovereignty of God. God has chosen to save us because of His great love. Without His grace and mercy, we would be hopelessly lost. Jonah stated it perfectly when he said, "Salvation comes from the LORD" (Jonah 2:9). When we're tempted to become proud of our position as the children of God, and we start to look down on the unsaved, we need to remember that we have done nothing to merit our salvation. We are saved only because we have placed our faith in Jesus Christ. This realization should humble us and cause us to love and honor our Savior even more.

They Were Angry

Christ's words struck at the heart of the pride and unbelief of the people in the synagogue. Suddenly, they saw themselves as they really were and they became defensive and angry. Luke 4:28–29 states, "All the people in the synagogue were furious when they heard this. They got up, drove him out of the town, and took him to the brow of the hill on which the town was built, in order to throw him down the cliff." The congregation was so enraged that they dragged Jesus outside the city and tried to kill Him.

Why were they so angry? I think that Augustine said it perfectly in his *Confessions:* "They love truth when it enlightens them. They hate truth when it accuses them. They love truth when it reveals itself and hate it when it reveals them." If Jesus had given this Jewish congregation a lovely devotional sermon about the brokenhearted and about the ministry of the coming Messiah, they would have welcomed Him with open arms. However, Jesus didn't preach that kind of sermon. He took the Word of God and applied it directly to people's hearts, convicting them of their sin. But this congregation didn't want their pride and prejudices exposed. They wanted soothing promises, not burning convictions. Why? Because they were proud and refused to yield to God.

Christians today need to be convicted of the sins that are grieving the Lord. However, some pastors are afraid to preach convicting sermons. They don't want to upset people and anger the members of the church. However, I would much rather have people become angry at my message than to be so complacent that they go on living in their sins.

How do you listen to a sermon? When you hear it, perhaps you immediately apply the message to the person next to you, saying, "Preach on, Pastor! My wife needs to hear what you're saying!" Or do you listen carefully and quietly, allowing the Lord to speak to you about your own life? The writer James has given us the formula for controlling our anger when we are under conviction. He stated, "My dear brothers, take note of this: Everyone should be quick to listen, slow to speak and slow to become angry, for man's anger does not bring about the righteous life that God desires" (James 1:19–20). We need to listen with open hearts and

99

minds, yielding our wills to the power and truth of God's inspired Word.

Jesus is the Great Physician (see Luke 4:23), and before the Lord can heal us, He must first diagnose the illness and prescribe the proper treatment. However, we must accept the diagnosis and treatment before healing can take place. And the treatment frequently is painful. Often He must wound us before He can heal us. But the pain He asks us to endure is minute compared to the wounds He suffered on the cross in our behalf (see Isa. 53:4–5). Not only does He heal us completely, but He pays the bill!

The congregation at Nazareth wasn't willing to accept the Lord's diagnosis of their prejudices and their pride. Instead of becoming angry at their own sin, their exclusiveness, jealousy, and pride, they became angry at God. As a result, they resisted the work of God and rejected the Son of God. Let's not make the same mistake. Let's humbly allow God's Word to expose our sin and rebellion and then bring us healing as we yield to Him. Let's willingly accept His correction and He will heal us.

9

An Angry Ruler

Most of us have a problem with anger, but people in leadership must be especially careful to keep their anger under control. Why? Because anger is not the best way to accomplish God's work. James 1:20 tells us that "man's anger does not bring about the righteous life that God desires." When spiritual leaders become angry, the work of the church suffers. The apostle Paul realized this and instructed the believers to choose men for the office of bishop who were "not quick-tempered" (Titus 1:7). While Paul was referring primarily to elders, pastors, and other church leaders, this requirement applies to any kind of leader. Because leaders are responsible for the lives and well-being of other people, it is vital that they learn how to exercise self-control.

In Luke 13 we read about a Jewish religious leader, the ruler of a synagogue, who had a serious problem with anger. He actually became angry with Jesus and didn't deal with his anger properly. Rather than coming to Jesus, he took out his anger on the congregation.

> On a Sabbath Jesus was teaching in one of the synagogues, and a woman was there who had been crippled by a spirit for eighteen years. She was bent over and could not

straighten up at all. When Jesus saw her, he called her forward and said to her, "Woman, you are set free from your infirmity." Then he put his hands on her, and immediately she straightened up and praised God.

Indignant because Jesus had healed on the Sabbath, the synagogue ruler said to the people, "There are six days for work. So come and be healed on those days, not on the Sabbath."

The Lord answered him, "You hypocrites! Doesn't each of you on the Sabbath untie his ox or donkey from the stall and lead it out to give it water? Then should not this woman, a daughter of Abraham, whom Satan has kept bound for eighteen long years, be set free on the Sabbath day from what bound her?"

When he said this, all his opponents were humiliated, but the people were delighted with all the wonderful things he was doing.

Luke 13:10–17

In order to understand this incident and why the ruler was angry, we must first understand the culture of that day. The ruler of the synagogue was not what we would consider to be a pastor. He was not the spiritual leader of the people. He was in charge of the public services in the synagogue, which meant choosing people to read the Scriptures and to lead the people in prayer. He also supervised the care of the building. It was his duty to see that the services started on time and that they were not interrupted. It was his job to make sure that everything was done decently and in order.

So, when Jesus interrupted the service and healed this woman, the ruler didn't stop to consider the woman and her needs. He was only concerned about conducting an orderly service, but Jesus had excited the people and upset the meeting. Even worse was the fact that Jesus had broken the Jewish law that forbade people to work on the Sabbath. So, in an effort to protect his own position of authority, the ruler became angry, scolding the people for breaking the traditional Sabbath law.

The ruler's response teaches us an important truth about anger: Anger is often a sign that we're covering up our own deficiencies. Frequently we use anger to hide the fact that we're lacking important inner qualities. As we look at this ruler, we see that his anger covered up at least four deficiencies in his life.

He Lacked Discernment

The ruler's first deficiency was a lack of discernment. He was unable to discern between good and evil and didn't even realize that God was in the synagogue! The ruler didn't recognize who Jesus was, that He was really God in the flesh. He treated Him rudely and accused Him of being a lawbreaker. When we examine the Scriptures closely, we discover that this was probably the last time Jesus taught publicly in the synagogue. At least it is the last record we have of His synagogue ministry. This incident took place just a few months before our Lord's crucifixion. Thanks to the blindness of the synagogue ruler, the people were deprived of the privilege of hearing Jesus continue to teach the Word in the synagogue one last time.

Imagine having the privilege of hearing Jesus teach in person, to hear the Word from the living Word Himself! This ruler had that opportunity, but he didn't take advantage of it. How do we know this? Because if he had really been listening to what Jesus said and had applied the Word to his life, he would not have responded as he did. If he had really taken God's Word to heart, it would have made him a better person, for the Word of God is light (Ps. 119:105). It shines into our hearts and dispels the darkness. The Word of God is food (Matt. 4:4; Heb. 5:12–14; 1 Peter 2:2). It comes into our souls and gives us nourishment. The Word of God is water (Eph. 5:26) that washes and cleanses the mind and the heart. The Word of God is seed (Luke 8:11). When it's planted and nurtured, it produces the fruit of the Spirit in us (Gal. 5:22–23). However, the ruler didn't receive any of these benefits because the Word never entered his heart. He was too busy with his responsibilities to recognize the fact that Jesus was no ordinary teacher. God was in his synagogue, and he didn't even notice.

Because this ruler lacked spiritual discernment, he couldn't see that Satan was also in the synagogue. His influence was present in the pain and restrictions of the crippled woman. Since the Lord Jesus didn't cast a demon out of the woman, we can assume that she was not demonized. However, the Scriptures describe her as having "a spirit of infirmity" (Luke 13:11 NKJV). Likewise, Jesus stated that the woman had been bound by Satan (see v. 16). This gives us the impression that Satan had somehow used a demonic force to cause this physical affliction; and because her affliction was controlled by Satan, no one had been able to cure her.

As I read this passage in Luke, I get the impression that this woman was not present when Jesus began teaching but that she arrived later. Coming in late to a service is embarrassing under normal conditions. And when we consider this woman's physical problems and the seating arrangement of the synagogue, her embarrassment was no doubt even more acute. Seating in the synagogue was carefully arranged, with the men on one side of the room and the women on the other. She probably sat at the back of the room so that no attention would be drawn to her handicap. Her illness had left her so crippled that she could no longer stand up straight. She was completely bent over, so she no doubt had a difficult time walking or even seeing where she was going. Her entrance into the synagogue more than likely elicited stares and hushed comments from the congregation.

How do you react when someone comes in late to a service, especially a person who looks or acts odd? If you're like most people, you're a bit irritated by the interruption. I imagine that this was the ruler's reaction. No doubt he saw this woman as she hobbled in, and he was probably angry at her for drawing attention away from the service. He probably thought to himself, "What is that woman doing here? Why can't she be on time like the rest of us!"

Jesus also would have seen this woman as she entered the room. Yet we don't find Him resenting her or what she did. Rather, He showed compassion and kindness toward her. He knew the hold that Satan had on her life, and He took immediate steps to release her from this oppression.

We can only imagine the suffering and pain that this woman had endured for eighteen long years. It would have been easy for her to become bitter and angry toward God for not answering her prayers for healing. Yet it doesn't appear that this woman did that. Despite the supreme effort it took for her to go anywhere, she came to the synagogue on the Sabbath to worship God. The passage gives no indication that the woman knew beforehand that Jesus would be in the synagogue or that she thought He could heal her. She didn't come to Him and beg to be healed. Jesus spoke to her first, calling her to come to Him. He then laid His hands on her and healed her (see vv. 12–13). Her prayers had been answered at last!

The ruler of the synagogue had the rare privilege of seeing and hearing God in the flesh. He had listened to the Word being taught as it had never been taught before. A miracle had been performed before his very eyes. Yet, instead of using this opportunity to glorify God, he became angry. Why? Because he lacked discernment.

He Lacked Power

The ruler's anger also revealed a lack of power in his life. He resented the fact that Jesus had usurped his authority in the synagogue. He was jealous of the power and authority that the Lord displayed. The ruler had been conducting the synagogue services for years. He had obeyed the Jewish law and traditions to the letter, yet his own spiritual life was dead. He certainly didn't have the power to defeat Satan and heal people; therefore, he felt threatened by what Jesus did. He fought off this threat to his pride and authority the only way he knew how—by getting angry.

When you read the ruler's response carefully, you realize just how senseless and absurd his statement really was. He told the people, "There are six days for work. So come and be healed on those days, not on the Sabbath" (Luke 13:14). But who would perform the healing? Was *he* going to do it? He couldn't be sure that Jesus would be there each time a person came to the synagogue to be healed. The statement was foolish.

Anger frequently leads us to say things that we later regret. A quick temper reveals to everyone just how weak we really are. When the ruler saw the power that Jesus possessed, he should have willingly admitted, "I have no power to heal anybody. The law has no power to change people. Our Jewish traditions and rituals are powerless. Only Jesus can save you and heal you." However, he didn't say this. Instead, he became angry, thinking that it would be a sign of his strength and authority; but it only showed the people how powerless and weak-willed he really was.

Like the ruler, so many religious people and groups today have "a form of godliness but [deny] its power" (2 Tim. 3:5). They're so concerned about their traditions and programs that they have no time for helping people. Likewise, we find few false religions running rescue missions or rehabilitation centers. Why? Because they have no message for lost sinners. They are powerless to help them. Instead of turning to the Lord, these groups continue to rely on their manmade traditions and false teachings, leading many people astray in the process. Even though Jesus healed this woman publicly as an example to everyone present, He did not treat her merely as an instrument to be used for His display of power. He saw her as an individual, not just as one of the crowd. He looked deep within her heart and saw the burden that she carried. He felt her need. He called to her, and He gently touched her and loosed her from her infirmity.

That word "loosed" (NKJV) is very important in this passage. In verse 15 Jesus said that these people would loose their oxen or donkeys to water them. Then why shouldn't this woman, a daughter of Abraham, made in the image of God, be loosed from this satanic bondage? The same word is used in both verses. Jesus clearly pointed out the ruler's lack of compassion, because he would treat an animal better than he would treat this woman.

Why did Jesus choose to expose this woman's need publicly? Instead of making her walk all the way to the front where everyone could see her, He could have gone to her after the service and quietly healed her. This would have seemed like a more logical approach, especially when we consider the fact that He was aware of the Jewish tradition forbidding any kind of work on the Sabbath. However, Jesus didn't try to hide either His power or His work. One reason why we don't see this kind of power in the church today may be that few Christians are willing to be open and honest about their faith. If more believers would simply do what Jesus wants them to do, without worrying about the possible consequences, great things could happen.

He Lacked Freedom

The ruler's anger revealed not only his lack of discernment and power but also his lack of freedom. If you had asked this man, "Are you free?" he would have quickly replied, "Of course I'm free! I'm a Jew, a son of Abraham, one of God's chosen people. We Jews have never been in bondage to anyone."

This was the prevailing attitude among the Jews of that day. They were extremely proud of their heritage and of the fact that they were God's chosen people. It seems strange, however, that they would even make such a statement when you consider their history. They had been ruled by various nations for hundreds of years. In the Book of Judges you find the Israelites under bondage to six different nations. Later, Babylon carried the Jews away into captivity. This was followed by bondage to the Medo-Persians and the Greeks. And even at this time in history, they were under Roman domination. But whenever the Lord confronted the Jews about their lack of freedom, they would hotly retort, "We are Abraham's descendants and have never been slaves of anyone" (John 8:33).

However, what these Jews didn't understand was that Jesus was not referring to physical or political bondage but rather slavery to sin. While the crippled woman was in physical bondage, the ruler of the synagogue was in a far worse state, for he was in spiritual bondage. Satan had so bound him

108

with traditions and laws that he couldn't even worship God freely. The Jews had added so many traditions to the Sabbath observance that the Sabbath had become a burden instead of a blessing.

God had originally ordained the Sabbath to be simply a day of physical rest for both people and animals. But then the Jews added their traditions to God's Law and changed God's gift into a form of bondage. The people were allowed to walk only a certain number of feet on the Sabbath. They had rules forbidding certain kinds of work on the Sabbath. If a person got a sliver in his finger, he could be punished for carrying a burden on the Sabbath. But if he removed the sliver, he would have broken one of the laws against working. The Jews spent so much time worrying about breaking a law, or looking for ways to get around the laws, that they had little time to enjoy the Sabbath.

The ruler of the synagogue was so concerned about man-made traditions that he ended up defending the Sabbath rather than the God of the Sabbath. He had forgotten the Lord's beautiful instructions to him in Micah 6:8: "He has showed you, O man, what is good. And what does the LORD require of you? To act justly and to love mercy and to walk humbly with your God." The ruler was certainly not being very just, merciful, or humble. When he saw the woman come in, he should have said, "Welcome, my friend. I see you have a great need. Why don't we all pause and ask Jehovah God to help you." But he didn't love God from his heart. Therefore, he was only concerned about maintaining his manmade traditions. He was also afraid of the people and of their reaction to Jesus. He was afraid of breaking out of the religious mold he was in. This ruler was in bondage to the Law, to tradition and to fear. His anger revealed his lack of freedom.

ANGRY PEOPLE

He Lacked Honesty

Finally, the ruler's anger revealed his lack of honesty. When the ruler scolded the people for coming to be healed on the Sabbath, Jesus called him a hypocrite (see Luke 13:15). In some texts the word *hypocrite* is plural. No doubt the ruler of the synagogue was not the only Jew present who bristled when the Lord healed this woman. Some probably looked at each other and said, "This man can't be from God. He wouldn't violate the Sabbath if He were truly a prophet of God." In fact, the passage indicates that more than one person opposed Jesus. But after the Lord had powerfully defended the woman and His actions, "all his opponents were humiliated" (v. 17).

Why did Jesus call the ruler a hypocrite? Because He knew that the man was only pretending spirituality and devotion to God. Hypocrites are people who deliberately deceive others, who try to make people think they're more spiritual than they really are. The word *hypocrite* comes from a Greek word that refers to a play actor or one who assumes a role. During the time of Christ, Greek actors would wear masks during their plays, and each mask represented a different character. Each time the actor changed his mask, the audience knew that a new character was speaking.

What an apt description of the ruler! Whenever he came into the synagogue, he put on his mask of spirituality and enforced the Law to the letter. However, outside the synagogue, he did as he pleased. But he couldn't hide his deception from Jesus. The Lord knew exactly what kind of person he was. He told the ruler, in effect, "You hypocrite! You will break the Sabbath laws at home in order to care for your animals, yet you refuse to bend the rules even a little in order to help a person in need. You pretend to defend the Law

110

while you continually break it yourself!" (see vv. 15–16). The ruler's anger was hypocritical and dishonest. He was not concerned about defending God or helping others; he was only concerned about defending his position of authority.

Not only was the ruler dishonest in his anger, but he was cowardly as well. In reality, the ruler was angry at Jesus, not at the people. He wanted to attack the Lord Jesus, but he was afraid to confront Him. So he lashed out at the people instead, saying, "There are six days for work. So come and be healed on those days . . ." (v. 14). But he really was talking to Jesus, and the Lord knew it.

Likewise, the ruler's anger revealed his unwillingness to love and to praise the Lord. Jesus had just performed a great miracle and the woman was standing before them completely healed. The congregation should have stood and joined her in singing praises to God. But, instead, the ruler and others became critical of Jesus for interrupting the service and for breaking their precious rules. But the Lord saw through their hypocrisy and exposed them for what they really were. "When he said this, all his opponents were humiliated, but the people were delighted with all the wonderful things he was doing" (v. 17).

While we should defend what we think is right, we must do so in love, humility, and kindness. Before we become angry at someone, we need to examine the reasons for our anger closely to make sure that we're not merely hiding our own deficiencies. We need to ask the Lord for the discernment to know when we should become angry and when we should not. We must be honest about our angry feelings and be willing to admit when we are wrong. We need to remember the freedom that we have in Christ and not try to enslave people with our traditions. And, most of all, we need to submit ourselves to the Lord and allow His power to flow through us, for only His power is strong enough to control the rage within us.

Whether we are leaders or not, we need to keep in mind the statement of James: "[M]an's anger does not bring about the righteous life that God desires" (James 1:20).

10

The Anger of Jesus

Many people have the mistaken idea that Christians should get along with everyone and never become angry at anyone. But the Scriptures clearly indicate that some forms of anger are not only justified, they are commanded. Those who condemn all forms of anger frequently point to Jesus as their example. However, you don't have to read very far in the New Testament before you discover that Jesus didn't get along with everybody, and that on several occasions, He even became angry with people.

Of course, Jesus is remembered most for His compassion for the fallen, the lost, the afflicted, the sorrowing, and the helpless. Indeed, He is a compassionate and loving God and Savior. However, we shouldn't forget His courage and His holy anger. God is light, as well as love, and He must express a holy indignation and anger toward sin. To do otherwise would deny both His holiness and His love. Pure and righteous anger is not a sign of sin but of love. Conviction without love leads to bigotry. Love without conviction is only sentimentality. But love plus conviction equals ministry. And this is what Jesus Christ displayed when He was here on earth.

Because Jesus loves us so much, He cannot tolerate evil in our lives. We should have this same attitude: "Let those who love the LORD hate evil . . ." (Ps. 97:10). Standing up for what is right frequently causes us to have enemies. Jesus didn't get along with everyone, and at times He had to express holy anger against sin and sinful people. He has set the example for us to follow in displaying our anger. He shows us the only reason for becoming angry—sin—and He shows us how to express that anger in constructive ways. Let's examine several incidents in the life of Christ to discover what sins in particular aroused His holy anger.

Hardness of Heart

When we look at the life and ministry of Jesus, we see Him expressing anger again and again at three different sins. The first sin that especially aroused His anger was the hardness of people's hearts. In Mark 3:1–7 we read:

> Another time he went into the synagogue, and a man with a shriveled hand was there. Some of them were looking for a reason to accuse Jesus, so they watched him closely to see if he would heal him on the Sabbath. Jesus said to the man with the shriveled hand, "Stand up in front of everyone."
>
> Then Jesus asked them, "Which is lawful on the Sabbath: to do good or to do evil, to save life or to kill?" But they remained silent.
>
> He looked around at them in anger and, deeply distressed at their stubborn hearts, said to the man, "Stretch out your hand." He stretched it out, and his hand was completely restored. Then the Pharisees went out and began to plot with the Herodians how they might kill Jesus.
>
> Jesus withdrew with his disciples to the lake.

114

Jesus saw the Pharisees' hardness of heart (see Luke 6:7), and it deeply grieved and angered Him. The word translated *hardness* in Mark 3:5 (NASB) is more accurately rendered "hardening." The process of hardening was occurring at that very time, and it grieved the Lord. These men were in the synagogue on the Sabbath Day, yet they were allowing their hearts to harden! Like the ruler of the synagogue in the previous study, these scribes and Pharisees had respect for Jewish tradition but no concern for a needy man. They were only using him as bait in their attempt to trap the Lord Jesus. Christ, on the other hand, saw this handicapped man as a person made in the image of God. He felt compassion for him and healed him. Nothing is more tragic than when we treat people as a means to an end and not as an end in themselves.

In this incident we see that the Pharisees' motive for being in the synagogue that day was wrong. They were not there to worship God or to learn His Word. They didn't believe they needed any more teaching. After all, they were very religious people. They studied the Scriptures and followed the Law to the letter. They prayed and tithed faithfully. They attended the synagogue services every Sabbath. Why were the scribes and Pharisees in the synagogue that day? They weren't there to listen to what Jesus had to say, because they had already rejected Him. They only came to watch Him and see what they could find to criticize.

Sadly, many Christians today are guilty of the same negative attitude. They don't attend church to worship God and to learn from His Word. They come to criticize and find something to gossip about. An incident in the life of Joseph Parker, the great British preacher, illustrates this fact. He was preaching at the City Temple in London, and after the service one of the listeners came up to him and said, "Dr. Parker, you made a grammatical error in your sermon today." He then proceeded to point out the error to the pastor. Joseph Parker looked at the man and said, "And what else did you get out of the message?" What a perfect rebuke! No one is perfect. Pastors, teachers, soloists, ushers— they all make mistakes. Occasionally, each one of us says or does the wrong thing (see James 3:2). This is natural. However, our reason for going to church is not to be critical of others but to worship the Lord and allow His message to speak to us. We should be concerned about ourselves and how we can serve the Lord better. A critical spirit has no place in the family of God. It only causes division and dissension.

Because their hearts were hard and unyielding, the scribes and Pharisees had no compassion for the man with the withered hand. They refused to listen to the Word of God. They became critical and angry and, as a result, brought God's judgment on themselves. This had been Israel's problem for centuries. Time and time again they had hardened their hearts against God and refused to obey Him. The prophet Zechariah knew this all too well:

> And the word of the LORD came again to Zechariah: "This is what the LORD Almighty says, 'Administer true justice; show mercy and compassion to one another. Do not oppress the widow or the fatherless, the alien or the poor. In your hearts do not think evil of each other.'
> "But they refused to pay attention; stubbornly they turned their backs and stopped up their ears. They made their hearts as hard as flint and would not listen to the law or to the words that the LORD Almighty had sent by his Spirit through the earlier prophets. So the LORD Almighty was very angry."
>
> Zechariah 7:8–12

The Lord Jesus was greatly grieved by the Pharisees' rebellious and stubborn attitude. He was angry at the way they treated the handicapped man and grieved at the way they were treating themselves and God. Mark 3:5 states that Jesus "looked around at them in anger." Notice the tense of the verbs in this passage. Christ's anger was not the slow, seething kind of anger that grows. It was a righteous indignation that was quickly aroused and was just as quickly quenched. However, the phrase "being grieved" (v. 5 NKJV) is a present participle. It indicates a continuous action. Thus, while Jesus was only angry at them for a moment, He constantly grieved over the hardening of their hearts. The same should be true of our anger. Our anger should be motivated by a deep and constant sense of grief at what sin is doing to others. While we should be angry at the sin, we should also feel sorrow for the sinner.

Jesus Christ is still grieving over the hardness of people's hearts. He sees in our assemblies people who listen to the Word of God just to find something to criticize, people who are not concerned about the needs of others, people who pretend to be righteous but resent it when others are blessed and helped by the power of God.

Notice how Jesus expressed His anger and grief. Rather than staying and arguing with the Pharisees, He simply left the synagogue (see v. 7). He knew that once people have rejected His truth and hardened their hearts against Him, all the arguments in the world will not change their minds. The Lord doesn't force Himself on us. If we don't want His truth and His salvation, He will go to someone who does. But it grieves Him greatly when people reject Him.

We must deal with our anger in the same way. Often the best solution is simply to walk away from the person with whom we are angry. This is especially true when the person has hardened his heart against us and against the Lord. In most cases, trying to reason with people does little good. Rather than trying to change people, we should simply forgive them and commit them to the Lord.

Pride

In Mark 10 we discover a second sin that angers the Lord Jesus, the sin of pride. The Lord will not tolerate pride because pride is born of selfishness. The only lasting cure for pride is for us to become like little children:

> People were bringing little children to Jesus to have him touch them, but the disciples rebuked them. When Jesus saw this, he was indignant. He said to them, "Let the little children come to me, and do not hinder them, for the kingdom of God belongs to such as these. I tell you the truth, anyone who will not receive the kingdom of God like a little child will never enter it." And he took the children in his arms, put his hands on them and blessed them.
>
> Mark 10:13–16

What a beautiful scene! In that day, it was customary for parents to bring their children to the rabbis for a blessing. In many places where Jesus stopped, He was met by parents who hoped to have their children blessed by Jesus. It's interesting to note that the word "them" in verse 13 is masculine. Many people have assumed that the mothers were the only ones who brought children to Jesus, but this passage indicates that the fathers also brought the little ones. I thank God for fathers who love the Lord and their children enough to raise their children to know Him. One of the greatest blessings we can receive is to have a father who knows the Lord, who prays, and who brings his children to Jesus.

We should also note that these parents were not bringing their children to Jesus to be baptized by Him. How do we know this? John 4:2 tells us that Jesus never baptized anyone, although His disciples frequently did. Considering the disciples' reaction to the parents in this incident in Mark 10, it's unlikely that the disciples ever baptized any children. In fact, the disciples scolded the parents for bothering Jesus with their children.

One of the things that I miss now that I'm no longer in pastoral ministry is the privilege of dedicating children and parents to the Lord. What a joy that parents bring children into the world and then dedicate them to the Lord's care and keeping! As I visit my former pastorates, I often meet many of the children that I dedicated. What a joy it is to see that they are serving the Lord now that they are adults.

When the parents brought their children to Jesus to be blessed, the disciples opposed them. Why? Because they were proud and thought they knew best. Instead of asking the Lord's will in the matter, they tried to handle the situation themselves, and they soon discovered that they had much to learn.

Why did the disciples become proud? Because they had wrong views about the Lord and about themselves. First, we see that they had a wrong view of the Lord's ministry. At this point in Christ's ministry, the disciples still didn't understand His purpose for coming to earth. They believed that Jesus would overthrow the Roman government and set up an earthly kingdom. They could see no reason for wasting time on children who would be of no use in such a kingdom. But the Lord told them, "Let the little children come to me, and do not hinder them, for the kingdom of God belongs to such as these" (Mark 10:14). The disciples were probably still pondering these words when a rich young ruler came to see Jesus (see vv. 17–22). Here was a man who had position, influence, and money. In the disciples' eyes, he was a valuable asset to the Lord's ministry. Yet Jesus refused to accept him as a disciple, and the disciples were perplexed. They still didn't understand the purpose of Christ's ministry. They couldn't see that Jesus was not concerned about a person's affluence. What mattered was his attitude. Was he humble or proud, needy or self-satisfied?

Unfortunately, many Christians today still make this same mistake. Because we don't understand the meaning of the kingdom of God, we give preferential treatment to certain people and ignore others, and often the children are neglected the most. I had this vividly illustrated to me as I was preaching in a church one Sunday. As I visited with the pastor between services, a group of children raced past us, laughing and having a good time. The pastor quickly apologized for their behavior, saying, "Brother Wiersbe, I'm sorry for all that commotion." I replied, "Don't apologize. Jesus would love it. After all, he's the One who threw the adults out of the temple and told the children to stay and sing their praises to God."

The disciples not only had a wrong view of the Lord's ministry and His kingdom, but they also had a wrong view of children. They thought that children were not important to the Lord Jesus. However, Christ has a high regard and a great love for children, and they are precious to Him. He was never too busy to spend time with them or to talk with them. In fact, He compared true believers to children on several occasions. He made it clear that people who wanted to follow Him had to become like little children (see v. 15). Jesus didn't mean that we should be childish, but childlike. Children are humble and dependent on their parents. Children are trusting and easily absorb what they are taught. Children are open-minded and eager to learn new things and have new experiences. They are always looking with wonder at what God does in His world. They see the best in everyone. This is the kind of faith that Christ wants us to have.

I imagine that the Lord is deeply grieved at the way children are treated today. Millions of children are destroyed before they have the opportunity to be born. Many children are being abused physically, mentally, and emotionally, and others are being ignored and neglected. At times, even believers have wrong attitudes toward children; they don't see them as important in the church. How tragic that churches make no real effort to bring lost children to the Lord. When they come to us and express a desire to accept Jesus, we often question whether they are old enough to understand such a commitment. What about you? Are you doing what you can to reach the children of the world for Christ? Jesus says to us, "Let the little children come to me, and do not hinder them . . ." (Mark 10:14). If we don't stand in their way, the children will naturally come to Jesus.

At the heart of the disciples' pride was the fact that they had a wrong view of themselves. They believed that they had the right to make decisions for the Lord. They thought they knew what was best for His ministry. So they proceeded to do things their own way and to ignore the Lord completely. Their pride and selfishness angered Jesus. In a graphic way He reminded them of the fact that "God opposes the proud but gives grace to the humble" (James 4:6).

Hypocrisy

Mark 11 records one of the best-known examples of Christ's anger. In this incident we find a sin that is very grievous to the Lord—hypocrisy.

121

On reaching Jerusalem, Jesus entered the temple area and began driving out those who were buying and selling there. He overturned the tables of the money changers and the benches of those selling doves, and would not allow anyone to carry merchandise through the temple courts. And as he taught them, he said, "Is it not written:
> 'My house will be called
> a house of prayer for all nations'?
> But you have made it 'a den of robbers.'"

The chief priests and the teachers of the law heard this and began looking for a way to kill him, for they feared him, because the whole crowd was amazed at his teaching.

Mark 11:15–18

Our Lord hates hypocrisy. When God gave the Law to the people of Israel, He also gave them detailed instructions on how He wanted them to worship Him. The Lord instituted the practice of animal sacrifice in order to prepare the people for the coming of the Messiah, the Lamb of God who would die for the sins of the world (see John 1:29). But, as they did with many of God's laws, the Israelites added stipulations and rules concerning sacrifices, and by the time of Christ, the Pharisees had turned the sacrificial system into big business. They required the people to purchase the animals from vendors at the temple at greatly inflated prices. The Jewish leaders used the worship services for their own gain. They became "storekeepers in the house of the Lord."

This was the situation that Jesus faced as He entered the temple that day. He didn't see a house of worship; He saw a religious supermarket. No wonder He was angry! The people had turned His holy temple and sacrifices into a religious racket. They turned God's house into a den of thieves (see v. 17). Jesus was reminding them of God's words to them in Jeremiah 7:11: "Has this house, which bears my Name, become a den of robbers to you? But I have been watching! declares the LORD." What is a den of robbers? It's the place where robbers run to hide after they've committed their crimes. Thus, Jesus was strongly condemning the people for their hypocrisy. The people were pretending to worship God when, in reality, they were only using the temple as a place to hide their sins.

Using the Lord's house as a place of business was bad enough if only the Jews had been involved, but they were giving a bad witness to the Gentiles as well. Why? Because the religious leaders were conducting their business in the Court of the Gentiles, where they should have been seeking to lead the Gentiles to a knowledge of the Lord. This court was the only area in the entire temple where the Gentiles could go to worship God. The Jews should have been there witnessing to the Gentiles, opening His Word to them, and sharing the truth of salvation. Instead, they were running a market and making money, but losing souls.

I wonder what the Lord would do today if He entered some of the buildings that house our churches and religious organizations? So many people today are using the name of Christ only to gain power, money, and influence. Their bad testimony is causing the unsaved to turn away from the truth of God. I'm sure God's greatest judgment is reserved for these religious racketeers; people who pose as holy and spiritual while they use their position and opportunities for personal gain.

Follow His Example

When is anger holy and constructive? When it's displayed according to the examples seen in the ministry of Jesus. While the Lord hates all sin, He is especially angry at the hidden sins of the heart, the sins we have just identified. He

123

is angered and grieved when people's hearts become so hard that they're unable to feel love and compassion for others. He hates a critical spirit. He is angry at selfish pride that causes us to hinder those who want to come to Him. And, most of all, Jesus hates hypocrisy. He is angered by people who pretend to be spiritual, who turn religion into a business and try to cover up their sins with pious prayers and other religious activities.

Hardness of heart, pride, hypocrisy—these are not only the sins of the unsaved but also of Christian people. The Lord will not tolerate deception in His children, and neither should we. We should be angered and grieved when we commit these sins or when we see them among God's people. This righteous anger should cause us to speak out against such sin and to seek to lead the sinners back to the Lord. When anger is displayed with love, humility, and self-control, the Lord will use it for our good and His glory.

We don't have the same accurate insight that Jesus has, so we must be careful to allow the Spirit and the Word to guide us. And we must spend much time in prayer lest we commit these sins ourselves while trying to help others! May the Lord give us all tender hearts, humble hearts, and honest hearts so that our lives will please the Lord and not grieve Him!

An Anthology
for Daily Reading

This anthology gathers together quotations from various people who have spoken and written about anger. I've tried to assess their thoughts through the teaching of the Word of God and apply them to the needs of Christian people like you and me. You may use this anthology as a daily devotional guide or you may refer to it as you have need.

1.

Better a patient man than a warrior,
   a man who controls his temper than one who takes
      a city.

Proverbs 16:32

The world's idea of "real manliness" is usually warped, but these false images go on, and mold young minds. (Solomon speaks about men, but what he says also applies to women.) The war hero and the Olympic winner are indeed heroes and deserve every bit of the recognition they receive, but what about the fake heroes manufactured by the entertainment world?

Better than being a brave soldier and taking a city is being a patient person and taking control of our temper. To conquer the enemy around us brings physical and political freedom, which is good, but to conquer the enemy within us brings moral and spiritual freedom, which is better. What good is it to enjoy political freedom if my will is in bondage, controlled by a vicious temper?

Pride is the sin that feeds the temper. Because we're "important," we get angry when people disagree with us and create problems for us. My wife and I were standing in line at a cafeteria when three men came in and pushed into the line ahead of us and even joked about it. Who were they that they had the right to get ahead of us! My first reaction was to say something sarcastic, but what would that have accomplished? Stooping to their level of rudeness wouldn't have made our lunch any more enjoyable.

Most people have never conquered a city, but many have done even better and conquered their own tempers and learned to control anger. "No, in all these things we are more than conquerors through him who loved us" (Rom. 8:37).

2.

To be angry is to revenge the fault of others upon ourselves.
Alexander Pope

This is just a poetic way of saying that we reap what we sow. The anger in my heart against somebody who has offended me doesn't really hurt the offender—it only hurts me. And if I go out to hurt my enemy, my anger will hurt me even more. Uncontrolled anger will usually do more damage to me than the original offense itself did to me.

All of which says that when we get angry we lose our perspective. Big things like love and kindness become very small, and small things like being important and having my own way suddenly become gigantic. That explains why "[a] quick-tempered man does foolish things . . ." (Prov. 14:17). David's anger against Nabal almost turned him into a murderer (see 1 Sam. 25), and Jesus warns us that our anger can make murderers out of us in our hearts (see Matt. 5:21-26).

Revenge is not "sweet"; it produces bitterness that can spread from family to family and generation to generation. Family feuds and ethnic wars have the same basic cause: a long memory and short temper are combined with an unforgiving spirit. To be able to say "I forgive you" and mean it can save us from a great deal of trouble and pain. To harbor resentment and plot revenge is to waste time and energy that could be used for more constructive activities.

Too often, anger in the heart spills over on people we really love and don't want to hurt. Bringing anger home from the workplace, or dragging anger to the workplace from home, only poisons the entire day and affects people who really shouldn't be involved in our problems. Better to humble ourselves, confess our sins, apologize, and make a new beginning. To nurture anger in our hearts is to feed the snake whose bite could kill us.

3.

Hatred stirs up dissension,
but love covers over all wrongs.
Proverbs 10:12

The last word in the verse is often the first thing in the situation: *wrongs*. Somebody wrongs us, we become angry, and this creates dissension. Great international conflicts usually start this way.

If a fellow believer wrongs me, my responsibility is to prayerfully speak to him or her about it and get it settled. Perhaps the offender didn't even realize what had been said or done and how it affected me. That's where love comes in, for "it [love] is not easily angered" (1 Cor. 13:5). Love puts the best interpretation on what others say and do and the motives behind those words and actions.

"Love covers over a multitude of sins," wrote Peter (1 Peter 4:8), quoting Proverbs 10:12. Led by the Spirit, he gave us a deeper understanding of the principle involved. Solomon's "all wrongs" becomes "a multitude of sins." My anger is a sin against the Lord, and if I nurture these angry feelings, I'll end up committing one sin after another. Anger is like a fire that spreads rapidly and can defile or destroy everything it touches. Anger sets our tongue on fire, and then angry words set our world on fire. "Consider what a great forest is set on fire by a small spark" (James 3:5).

"A gentle answer turns away wrath, but a harsh word stirs up anger" (Prov. 15:1). If we have the love of God in our hearts (see Rom. 5:5), we can quickly ask the Holy Spirit to help us speak that kind word and cover that wrong with for-giveness. Returning evil for evil only makes matters worse. That gentle loving word that reveals compassion and con-cern is like a spring rain that puts out a fire. By nature, we want to fight back and assert our rights, but the Spirit of God enables us to act not like ourselves but like Jesus.

Don't live on a battleground. Turn it into a garden.

4.

People who fly into a rage always make a bad landing.
Will Rogers

One Easter evening, I was flying from Detroit to Chicago, and when our plane touched down on the runway, we "bounced" a couple of times and then taxied to our gate. Our flight attendant was ready for the situation and came on the PA system saying, "That was our Easter Sunday evening hippity-hop bunny landing. Welcome to Chicago!" We passengers laughed instead of complained.

To go ballistic and fly into a rage is the best way to set the stage for a few bounces if not a crash landing. "What's so bad about losing my temper?" a parishioner asked the pastor. "I explode and then it's over."

"So does a volcano explode," the pastor replied, "but think of the damage that's left behind."

When my wife and I arrive at a city for ministry, our host often asks, "Did you have a good flight?" My reply is usually, "Any flight that takes off safely and lands safely is a good flight." Whether or not the food was good or the flight smooth is really irrelevant. We got there safely!

The next time you're tempted to fly into a rage and tell somebody off, picture yourself as a pilot and ask yourself, "What kind of landing will I have?" Yes, it sometimes feels good to give vent to your anger, but what will be there after you land? Will it be a bumpy landing, a crash landing, or a smooth landing?

"A hot-tempered man must pay the penalty . . ." (Prov. 19:19). Don't let your temper be the pilot.

5.

Anger is never without a reason, but seldom with a good one.

Benjamin Franklin

Once the fire of our anger starts to grow, the emotional smoke it generates clouds our mind and defiles our conscience and we start thinking and doing dumb things. We find it very easy to condemn our enemy and justify ourselves. We convince ourselves that our anger is appropriate and that we have every right to display it. Ralph Waldo Emerson wrote in his journal, "We do what we can, and then make a theory to prove our performance the best." Today's counselors call this "rationalizing."

The minute we start condemning others and defending our anger, we give evidence that we've forgotten the mercy of God. Suppose the Father treated us the way we treat others? Because of what Jesus did for us on the cross, God in His mercy doesn't give us what we do deserve, and in His grace He gives us what we don't deserve. There have been times in our lives when the Father could have chastened us severely, but He didn't. "[He] does not treat us as our sins deserve or repay us according to our iniquities" (Ps. 103:10).

Yes, there's a time for righteous anger, but let's be sure it's *righteous*. And let's also be sure we handle it the right way and seek to let God bring good out of evil. Fire in a fireplace is a good thing, but let it out of the fireplace and you'll turn your house to ashes. "Like a city whose walls are broken down is a man who lacks self-control" (Prov. 25:28). When the walls are broken down, anything can get out—and anything can get in!

Angry people find it difficult to be "reasonable." They're too worked up to think logically, listen patiently, or speak reasonably. To be controlled by sinful anger is like trying to drive a truck down a steep incline at eighty miles an hour, without brakes or a steering wheel.

Yes, you and I can excuse and explain our anger and make our defense sound reasonable, but deep inside we know we're just fooling ourselves. Our thoughts aren't always God's thoughts, and so we need to pause to consider His Word and His will. The Lord asks us as He asked Jonah, "Have you any right to be angry?" (Jonah 4:4). Will we give Him an honest answer?

130

6.

> I want men everywhere to lift up holy hands in prayer,
> without anger or disputing.
>
> 1 Timothy 2:8

Anger is both a thermometer and a thermostat: It controls our "moral temperature" but it also reveals it. Just as steel is tempered to give it strength, so God gives us temper so we have courage to face evil. It's when we lose our temper and get angry that we become weak. The person who can't become angry at sin and injustice is lacking moral quality, because godly anger is an awesome weapon for fighting sin. But our anger also lets people know when the wrong fire is burning inside and when something is missing in our spiritual walk.

Paul informs us that anger and disputing can hinder our praying. The holy hands we lift to God must be open and clean, ready to receive His answers. When those hands become fists, our prayers won't be answered.

The Lord's Prayer begins with "Our Father," not "My Father" (Matt. 6:9), and there are no singular personal pronouns in the prayer that refer to God's people. All the pronouns are plural: "*Our* Father . . . Give *us* . . . Forgive *us* . . . lead *us* not into temptation . . . deliver *us* . . ." (Matt. 6:9–13). We can pray in solitude but we never pray alone. All of God's people in the family of faith are a part of our prayers whether we realize it or not. I have no right to ask God for anything for my life that would create problems for your life, because we belong to each other and need each other.

But what about the "angry prayers" in the Book of Psalms, what the theologians call "the imprecatory psalms"? They surely aren't examples of "family prayers," are they? No, but some of these psalms are "official prayers" brought by

131

King David to the Lord on behalf of the people of Israel. The language may shock us, but we must remember that David is angry at sin and sinful people who wanted to destroy Israel. If Israel had been destroyed, the world would have no Bible and no Savior. Anger is one thing, but anguish is quite another. Anguish is anger mixed with love in a heart that's broken because of the sins of humanity. The tearful anger that Jeremiah and Jesus showed was anguish. They experienced no joy in announcing the doom of their enemies.

The psalmists' prayers were based on the terms of God's covenant with Abraham in Genesis 12:1–3 and His covenant with Israel, found in Leviticus 26 and Deuteronomy 27–28. The Lord promised to defeat Israel's enemies if Israel obeyed Him, and the psalmists were only asking God to keep His promises. By the way, there are also "imprecatory" statements in the New Testament, such as Matthew 23 and Luke 11:37–52 (spoken by Jesus), Galatians 1:6–9 (spoken by Paul), Revelation 6:10 (spoken by saints in heaven), Revelation 18:6–8, 20 (spoken by an angel from heaven), and Revelation 19:1–6 (spoken by the multitudes in heaven).

7.

My dear brothers, take note of this: Everyone should be quick to listen, slow to speak and slow to become angry, for man's anger does not bring about the righteous life that God desires.

James 1:19–20

"The reason we have two ears and only one mouth is that we may listen the more and talk the less." The philosopher Zeno of Citium said that three centuries before Christ was born, but it's just as true today.

Our ears should be tuned to what others are saying and what their words reveal about their feelings. Too often we're so busy thinking about what we plan to say next that we don't pay close attention to what others are saying to us. This bad habit is not only insulting, it's also dangerous.

It's remarkable how people start to calm down and begin acting friendlier when they discover that we're actually listening to them and not interrupting. We let them speak until they finish, and when they're finished, we don't answer immediately. Rather, we show them that we're pondering their words, and then we tell them what we agree with. We might even reflect back to them how we sense that they feel or how we interpret what they said. That's what it means to be "quick to listen."

As we listen and wait, we have time to pray and ask God for grace to be loving and speak kind words. Some people have short fuses and if we don't seek God's help immediately, they'll say something that will do damage to the cause of Christ. What good is it to win an argument and lose an opportunity to glorify Christ and promote the righteousness of God?

"Do not be quickly provoked in your spirit, for anger resides in the lap of fools" (Eccles. 7:9). The fruit of the Spirit is "love . . . gentleness and self-control" (Gal. 5:22–23), the very qualities we need so we can listen patiently and reply in a Christlike manner. The important thing is not that our opponents agree with us but that all of us agree with the Lord. That soft answer still works!

8.

"Don't get mad—get even."
Anonymous

> Do not repay anyone evil for evil . . . Do not take revenge,
> my friends, but leave room for God's wrath, for it is written:
> "It is mine to avenge; I will repay," says the Lord. On the
> contrary:
>> "If your enemy is hungry, feed him;
>>> if he is thirsty, give him something to drink.
>> In doing this, you will heap burning coals on his head."
> Do not be overcome by evil, but overcome evil with good.
>
> Romans 12:17–21

If you have the ability not to get mad, you probably also have the ability not to want to get even, so cultivate the positive approach. If contemplating your revenge gives you the strength to smile and temporarily let things pass, then your heart is controlled by the wrong motives.

I knew a man who kept a little book containing the names of people who had (he thought) insulted him or embarrassed him, including people in church who had lovingly disagreed with some of his ideas. He was one of the most miserable men I have ever met. You can't be filled with love if your heart is dedicated to revenge.

Faith, hope, and love are the three important marks of the Christian life. But if we live to get even, those three graces will never be seen in us. Certainly a craving for revenge would drive the love out of our hearts, for we're commanded to love even our enemies (see Matt. 5:43–48). If we truly love someone, we have hope that they will enjoy the blessing of God and grow in grace. We will want the very best for them. But a desire for revenge would automatically cancel that kind of hope.

"But you're asking me to take my hands off and just let things fall apart!" you may argue. No, *God* is asking us to take our hands off and trust him to solve the problem and balance the books. That's where faith comes in. Our plans to avenge ourselves mean we don't really believe His promise in Romans 12:17–21, so our faith is also gone! Is it really worth it to lose faith, hope, and love just so we can hurt somebody else?

The phrase "get even" is definitely not Christian, for Christians must rise above the level of their enemies. To "get even" puts us on the same level as they are, and that's not where Christians are supposed to be! We have to live on a higher plane and let God handle these problems for us. "In taking revenge," wrote Francis Bacon, "a man is but even with his enemy; but in passing it over, he is superior."

Have we asked the Lord to provide us with opportunities to give food and drink to those who hate us?

9.

"I have no more right as a Christian to allow a bad temper to dwell in me than I have to allow the devil himself to dwell there."

Charles Haddon Spurgeon

"But woe to the earth and the sea,
    because the devil has gone down to you!
He is filled with fury,
    because he knows that his time is short."

Revelation 12:12

Satan is God's enemy and our enemy, and he is very angry. God is love, but Satan is fury and hatred. He's a roaring lion seeking to devour us (1 Peter 5:8) and a subtle serpent trying to deceive us (2 Cor. 11:3). He hates God's people and tries to get God's people to hate each other.

Of course, when Satan first approaches his victims, he masquerades as a friend who wants to give help. That's the way he approached Eve, offering to give her what the Lord had held back from her. Eve didn't detect a trace of anger in Satan's voice, but behind the façade was an enemy who wanted to separate her and Adam from the presence of the Lord. No matter what the enemy says to you or offers you, he is still an enemy.

Anger in our hearts gives Satan a foothold in our lives. Paul wrote, "In your anger do not sin: . . . and do not give the devil a foothold" (Eph. 4:26–27). Love draws us closer to God, for God is love, but anger opens the door to the devil. When we cultivate a bad temper and defend it, or carry a grudge and refuse to confess it, we make it easier for Satan to take control of our lives. Satan rejoices when he sees a heart filled with anger, for unholy anger is an awesome weapon in the devil's hands for weakening and destroying the work of the Lord.

Satan is an accuser (Rev. 12:10), and when we have anger in our hearts, we find ourselves slandering God's people and spreading gossip about them. Satan is a liar (John 8:44), and anger can turn us into liars. Hidden anger is a subtle transformer of character, and Satan uses it to his advantage, especially in believers who are in places of leadership in the church.

"We know that anyone born of God does not continue to sin; the one who was born of God keeps him safe, and the evil one cannot harm him" (1 John 5:18). Jesus Christ has conquered the devil and his hosts, and if we abide in Christ, Satan can't reach us. But if we nurture ill will and anger in our hearts, we're only inviting Satan to take over. Confess that anger immediately and claim God's forgiveness, and then you will be free to love God and serve His people in humility and love.

10.

Therefore, if you are offering your gift at the altar and there remember that your brother has something against

you, leave your gift there in front of the altar. First go and
be reconciled to your brother; then come and offer your gift.

Matthew 5:23–24

"How good and pleasant it is when brothers live together
in unity!" (Ps. 133:1). But as the familiar jingle puts it

> To live above, with saints we love,
> Will certainly be glory.
> To live below, with saints we know—
> Well, that's another story!

As important as worship is to the spiritual life, Jesus said
that reconciliation with my brother is even more important.
"If anyone says, 'I love God,' yet hates his brother, he is a liar.
For anyone who does not love his brother, whom he has seen,
cannot love God, whom he has not seen" (1 John 4:20).

When we come to the altar with our gifts and worship,
God sees our hearts and knows what is there. If I know
there's a barrier between me and another believer, and I
do nothing about it, that barrier will come between me and
the Lord. "If I had cherished sin in my heart, the Lord would
not have listened . . ." (Ps. 66:18). How can we worship God
from our hearts if our hearts are not right?

I recall a day when I was at my desk, preparing a sermon,
and the Lord convicted me from the very Scriptures I was
studying. "You can't preach this sermon," He told me,
"because you haven't really obeyed it." So I confessed my
sin, picked up the phone, and settled the matter with my
brother. It was important to prepare the message, but it was
even more important to prepare *the messenger.*

The Old Testament priests couldn't go into the holy place
unless first they stopped at the laver and washed their hands
and their feet. If they failed to do this, they might die! When
we come to Christ with our worship and offerings, we need

137

to be sure there's no anger in our hearts, no unconfessed sins, no memories of bad relationships with our brothers and sisters. And it isn't enough just to confess these things to the Lord. We should also go to the offended brother or sister and make matters right.

Jesus teaches us to worship God "in spirit and in truth" (John 4:24). That's the kind of worshipers the Father is seeking. Do we qualify?

Warren W. Wiersbe is Distinguished Professor of Preaching at Grand Rapids Baptist Seminary and has pastored churches in Indiana, Kentucky, and Illinois (Chicago's historic Moody Church). He is the author of more than 150 books, including *God Isn't in a Hurry, The Bumps Are What You Climb On,* and *The Bible Exposition Commentary* (2 vols.).